MILLEA & Co T

MILLEA & Co
TAILORS &
OUTFITTERS

MILLEA & Co

MAIN STREET
TIPPERARY

Main Street, Tipperary (Lawrence Collection, National Library)

Dedicated to our children

First published 1977 by
The Appletree Press Limited
6 Dublin Road Belfast BT2 7HL

Designed by
Spring Graphics Co.

Printed by
The Appletree Press Ltd
4 Marcus Ward Street Belfast BT7 1AP

Cloth ISBN 0 904651 24 X
Paper ISBN 0 904651 23 1

Faces of Munster

Seán McMahon & Art Ó Broin

Contents

Preface 6

Introduction 7

WORK AND LEISURE 9

CITY TOWN AND COUNTRY 33

TROUBLES 63

JOURNEYS 81

Index of Authors 95

Acknowledgements 95

Select Bibliography 95

Preface

Our thanks are due to the director and staff of the National Library of
Ireland, the staff of the Library of the Institute of Continuing Education (NUU)
Magee College, Derry, especially Alan Roberts; the staff of the Belfast Central
Library; Michael Coady of Carrick-on-Suir; Diarmuid O'Donavan of Cork; T H
Murphy of Castleisland; James Clancy and Senan Rush of Kilrush; Liam Hogan
of Ennis; John Galvin of the County Library, Tralee; Edmund Flaherty of
Clontarf; Brud Slattery of Lahinch; Donnchadh O Suilleabhain, Secretary of
the Oireachtas; Jim O'Neill Librarian, *Cork Examiner*; Frank D'Arcy of Derry.

Introduction

Comparisons, as a well-known, non-RIC constable once remarked, are odorous; they are also inevitable. When one comes to contemplate the face of Munster after gazing with fascinated eyes at the West for a year or so one cannot but be struck at the differences. However arbitrary the division of the country into provinces may once have been, allowing for the ambivalence of a man from northwest Clare or east Waterford, they grew into self-conscious entities. Certainly the Munster of eighty years ago presents a different mien to the time-traveller than that of Ulster or Connacht; or perhaps one should say that the available materials with which an impression of that Munster may be built give a picture which is different.

This book follows the pattern of its predecessors, *Faces of the Past* and *Faces of the West* and attempts to present a view of the southern province's past by the marriage—sometimes shot-gun wedding—of the distinct sources, the photographs and the literature of the period. One medium, by itself, might tend towards bias but the camera which had not yet learned to lie and the piece of imaginative literature as abstract and brief chroniclers of the time, set in opposition to each other, so to speak, may together hope to produce a more complete picture of the time.

The face of Munster as it appears in wet-plates and print is one of two great contrasts, richness and turbulence. The fields seem bigger, the roads wider and straighter, the mountains higher, the towns more populous, the people more comfortable than in the West. There is a city at once sedate and rebellious, able to contain within its extension all kinds of dissonances. There is

Protest demonstration in Cork in the 1920s. (Photo; courtesy J Cluskey)

7

urban sophistication and a sense of rural plenty and the impression that the people had time to spare from the the grind of survival—old men to see visions, young men to dream dreams. Fenianism and Republicanism run like green threads through the region's history. One becomes conscious of a country worth fighting for; and civil war seems more bitter here.

Unlike the western province there are no great writers here if one excludes the elusive George Fitzmaurice and the Munster half of Somerville and Ross. Yet there are many whose names to any generation but the present one were, as Parnell once said of Tom Kettle, household words. Charles Kickham, Canon Sheehan, An tAthair Peadar, the Sullivan brothers, William O'Brien, used fill our grandparents' bookshelves. They tended, on the whole, to reflect the rural scene rather than the urban. Cork's recurring golden ages have great gaps between them and there are few writers worth consideration between the time of Milliken and Mahoney and that of Daniel Corkery. For the full celebration of Cork's patchy urbanity you have to wait for Sean O'Faolain and Frank O'Connor. Contrariwise Youghal and Waterford have figured in better than average novels of the period by William Buckley and Katherine Cecil Thurston. Limerick had its own poetic child in Michael Hogan, the Bard of Thomond, whose woodnotes wild tended at times to grow sharp. There were none of the great originals like Yeats and Moore and Hyde; yet the Gaelic revival would have been rather different without An tAthair Peadar, Beirt Fhear and Ballingeary Teachers College, and the development of the theatre in Ireland would have suffered without such shapers as T C Murray and Lennox Robinson.

As for the pictures they are dominated by the work of Robert French whose elegant and unmistakeable photographs taken for his employer Lawrence have become one of the main resources of the social researcher of the period. We have also included some Lawrence photographs from a period earlier than when French was his main journeyman. These were originally stereograms, pairs of almost identical pictures to be viewed though Sir Charles Wheatstone's stereoscope to obtain a three-dimensional image. Most Victorian drawing-rooms had these and many a month of rainy Sundays was whiled away with them. The other great archive of Munster pictures of the period is the Cork Examiner Collection which consists of many boxes of mainly uncatalogued plates. One cannot help but be conscious of the daily disappearance of much excellent material through age accident or spring-cleaning. One would recommend to UCC or the Cork Municipal Art Gallery or some such agency to follow the lead in this matter of the Public Records Office in Belfast and the Learning Resource Centre at Magee College, Derry. They have done what they can to encourage local people to search through their attics and albums so that precious and unique records of a past age may be copied and preserved. We have been conscious in this compilation that just as history was the story of the past as told by the winners, now it is built of what archives survive.

ART Ó BROIN & SEÁN McMAHON

Work & Leisure

Verandah, Eccles Hotel, Glenariff, Co. Cork (Lawrence Collection, National Library)

They now reached a low swing-gate, painted white. A couple of men sprang, apparently, out of the ditch, to open and hold it. They passed through, and on to what was like another road, only narrower than that which they had left, and running through a field. After a minute or two they turned a corner, and a huge square white house, well lighted up, stood at the top of a wide field before them. A little white railing ran on each side of the grass as they approached, and marked off the sweep before the door.

As soon as the sound of the car was heard in the house, the hall door was thrown wide open, letting out a stream of light and noise, and mingled odors of all sorts, the basis of which was turf smoke; and a crowd rushed out to welcome the visitors. A half-dozen or more daughters, some grown up and others as yet in the chrysalis stage, seized on Dicky. Then they all bustled in; and in the hall, where was burning a huge fire of peats, Hogan was introduced to his hostess, a comely matron, with an amiable, good-humoured face,—a Kerry woman, as evidenced by her accent, and with the fine dark eyes and hair so often seen in that favoured district. Hogan and Dicky now followed a barefooted girl up to their rooms, which blazing turf fires made agreeable and homelike after the chilly journey.

May Laffan *Hogan M P* (London, 1896)

MAY HARTLEY (nee Laffan) though born in Dublin, really hailed from Cashel, Co. Tipperary. Best known as the author of slum sketches, *Flitters, Tatters and the Counsellor* she also wrote *Hogan MP* in 1876, a fairly scathing attack on the inadequacies of catholic education. It gives a rare and excellent account of the emerging native middle class.

Coole House, Millstreet, Co. Cork (Lawrence Collection, National Library)

. . . ní raibh an "Gioblachán" sásta fós. Thóg se anuas fidil bhí ar crocadh, de'n bhalla, agus chuir sé i gcóir í.

"An dtaithneann ceól leat?" ar seisean.

"Taithneann go maith," arsa mise, "Ta spéis mhór agam ann i gcómhnuidhe."

"Má's mar sin atá an sgéal," ar sé, "gheobhaidh tú ceól anois nó ríamh."

"Má tá sé mar an ceól do thug an mac alla uaidh ó cíanaibh ná bac leis."

"Éist," ar seisean, ag leigint gáire as, "agus tabhair do bhreith nuair táim críochnuighthe."

Tosnuigh sé ag seinm, agus dá mbéinn ag caint go ceann seachtmhaine ní fhéadfainn tuarasgbháil cheart do thabhairt ar an cóimhsheinm d'éirigh san uaimh. B'áluinn an bhleidhleadóir an "Gioblachán" agus bhí sé 'n-a chumas, "o neart na taithíghe," is dócha, ceól do bhaint as an mac alla chómh maith leis an bhfidil. Dá mbéadh gach éin-ghléas ceól i n-Éirinn bailighte isteach i n-éan-halla amháin agus íad go léir ar siubhal i n-éinfheacht, ní fheadfadh síad céol níos binne ná níos áilne ná níos taithneamháighe do thabhairt uatha ná an ceól do thug an fhidil agus an mac alla dhúinn an óidhche úd. Thóg sé an cróidhe agus an t-anam asam. Níor mhothúigheas pían ná tuirse ná eagla ná éinnídh eile acht amháin aoibhneas agus sásamh aignidh an fhaid do bhí an "Gioblachán" ag seinm agus d'fhanfainn annsoin ag éisteacht leis ar feadh lae agus óidhche gan bheith tuirseach dhe.

Tomás Ó hAodha, *An Gioblachan* (Dublin, 1903)

TOMÁS Ó hAODHA was born in Milltown Malbay, Co. Clare in 1866, the son of a cooper. He became a teacher in 1886 in Dublin and was one of the early members of the Gaelic League. His greatest interest was in Irish music and in the teaching of Irish song in which he was an innovator. He wrote plays and short stories; the piece is from his novel *An Gioblachán*. He died in 1935.

An Gioblachán (Lawrence Collection, National Library) 11

Then, "He's away!" signalled from the lower end—a thundering charge of horses to the gateway, long ere there was time to get out of covert. Peter felt the reins almost wrenched from his grasp, Starlight tearing on, until his career was checked by bumping into a mass of horses jumbled into the narrow gateway, their paths barred by an enraged field master who had pulled his across the way. Hounds dashed out of covert, settling to the line; the field master fled with a clear lead, and the checked flood poured out, hustling and voluble. The pack were tearing down the hillside; and, judging by the yells which drifted across, the fox was making his way up the steep hill beyond the road. There were two ways to get down—one direct, embellished by a crop of jutting-out rocks, and so steep that horses slid on their tails; the other to the left, across a low bank, and down a more gradual slope. Fortunately for himself Peter chose the longer way, for, as he charged the bank, he felt very much as if the grey had turned into a four-legged motor, with the brake out of

order. His great Roman nose to the earth, Starlight thundered downwards, slid through a broken fence, and dashed at the wall fencing the road. Here Peter saw a fleeting vision of sound macadam, touched once, and another of an awkward stick of timber, vanishing, badly rapped, beneath him. This was mixed up with a third fleeting view of other horses, scuttling from his onslaught, and a faint peppering of comments, not precisely complimentary, echoing as he fled.

Hounds were slipping out of sight over a high green bank, flanking a whitewashed chapel and a churchyard. The men in front turned to the left; the grey, not Peter, turned after them over a thorny fence, half hedge, half wall, at which Starlight checked, and then took with a bucking lurch which set Peter's perfectly clad legs flapping widely, to find rest on his horse's neck. Also he thought he heard a chuckle somewhere behind him.

Pink coats in front began to drop out of sight into a narrow lane, pausing cautiously as they slid down, but

UHC Foxhounds at Fermoy Old Barracks on 17 March 1899 (Photo J Thompson, Fermoy: Crawford Municipal School of Art Collection, Cork)

12

here fortunately, though he tore up to it, Starlight steadied himself, and just as Peter, his lips set grimly for the crash, was wondering whether his grave would be the well of a passing car, or the inside of an approaching governess cart, the grey propped, spun round, again laying Peter on his mane, sliding down the now broken bank with the steadiness of a trained hunter. Over fresh, a start down-hill—it must be only that; so he rode on with the crowd, dubiously.

Hounds had checked among the tombstones and were spread out, noses to earth, over the humping graves. "Twas a place for a sphortin' man to lie," observed a capped countryman by Peter's side. "With the fox crossin' in near ivery run from Doleen."

"See him across?" thundered the Master, peering down from the high fence above the graves.

A man with a spade hustled round from behind the chapel, waving the weapon of his gruesome toil, and indicating the line. "He wint over me very head," he cried, "ann' I diggin' Timsy Phelan's grave to be ready to-morry. Cleared it out, an' I seen him away goin' esht by Martin Hanlon's shlate house."

Dorothea Conyers, *Peter's Pedigree* (London 1904)

DOROTHEA CONYERS (born Miss Blood Smith in Limerick in 1871) was after Somerville and Ross the laureate of huntin' Ireland. Her stories are racy, funny and full of exterior characterisation of the 'types' associated with her material. She made no attempt to penentrate more deeply into character nor to examine closely the relationship between her Anglo-Irish protagonists and the 'peasantry'. *Peter's Pedigree* (1904) is one of the best of her stories and may be summed up as it was at the time of publication, 'Hunting, horse-dealing, and love-making in Co. Cork.'

DAN. Yeh, man, don't be talking like that a day like this! There isn't a mother's soul in this parish but yourself that wouldn't be out of his mind with delight this minute, and everyone to be praising his own flesh and blood! *(To Maura.)* I'm sorry in my soul you didn't see the match, Mrs. Morrissey. I nearly killed the little mare and killed myself hurrying back from the town to see if I could see even the end of it. An' 'twas a grand sight surely.

MAURA. Wisha, God help us, Dan, I'm a bit too old now to be going places like that.

DAN. Wisha indeed, and indeed you're not, ma'am. A person would think the way you talk you were drawing the pension. But sure whatever excuse there was for you there was none at all for himself here.

BAT. We'd look well, begor. Maura an' myself, going to yer tournament! *(laughs derisively)*.

DAN. An' why not, Bat? Why not? The sight o' your son to-day would be giving you a kind of feeling, maybe, that your best cows and your heaviest pigs could never give you.

BAT *(shaking his head)*. God help you, Dan Hegarty! An' you a young man just beginning to rear a little family!

DAN. If I am then, Bat Morrissey, I only wish to God one o' them would grow up something like your Hugh! So I would. *(To Maura.)* All the people, and the strangers even, were cheering like mad for him. Half a dozen times you's be seeing the ball it flying into the goal posts, an' your heart would be in your mouth, thinking the other side had the goal, when you'd see him sending it back again with a puck into the middle of the field. 'Twas like a miracle the way he used to save it every time!

MAURA. Well! well!

DAN. I galloped away when it was over as I wanted to clear away before the crowds, but I gave one look back, an' they were shouldering him, an' cheering mad, an' shouting for him as if it was a member of Parliament he was.

BAT. An' for what now?

14 DAN *(with a gasp)*. For what?

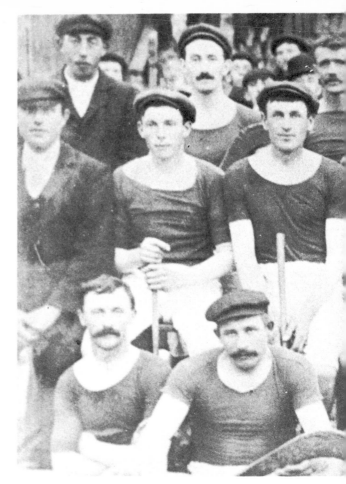

BAT. Yes, for what, Dan Hegarty?

DAN. Didn't I tell you.

BAT. Is it because he hit a bit of a leather balleen with a twisted stick? Tch! tch! tch! *(standing up and going towards room)*. 'Tis thinking I am that half the world is becoming a pack o' fools! *(goes into room)*.

MAURA *(confidentially)*. I'd know could you tell me was he hurt at all, Dan?

DAN, I don't know then—I don't think so . . . .I'm almost sure he wasn't, now that I think of it.

MAURA. Thanks be to the Almighty God an' his Blessed Mother for that!

T C Murray, *Birthright* (Dublin, 1911)

Clonea (Co. Waterford) Senior Hurling Champions, 1902
(Willie Flynn/Carrick Society)

THOMAS CORNELIUS MURRAY was born in Macroom in 1873 and became a teacher in Dublin in 1893. From 1909 he contributed many plays to the Abbey, the best and most successful being *Autumn Fire* (1924) with a plot as old as *Phaedra*. The realism of his West Cork dialogue and the daring choice of some of his themes caused him some clerical opposition at home and he was glad to transfer to the Model Schools at Inchicore. *Birthright (1910) is typical of his mise-en-scene* and preoccupations. It tells of family rivalry between two brothers for the attention of their parents and the possession of the farm. Yeats called it as 'perfect as a Chopin Prelude'. Murray died in 1959.

The game of hurling remained popular in rural areas of the south despite the anglicisation of much of Irish life by the end of the nineteenth century. The founding of the Gaelic Athletic Association by Michael Cusack (at Thurles in 1884) to organise and spread the game, was the natural outcome of the awakening sense of nationality of the period. In turn members of the GAA were to make an important contrioution to the revolutionary movement.

KILKEE-THE-GRAND

Nor sea nor shore, by artist planned
No lauded scene, nor fairyland—
Not austral flood by coral strand,
Nor where the Sun doth Night command,
The purple tide by gods adored,
The climes Genoa's lord explored,
Nor region brighter—can afford,
Thy glory pale Kilkee-the-grand!

The Titan King, from pole to pole,
The sceptre sways without control.
His tide on countless strands doth roll,
Whose pride all times and tongues extol.
To Maghar from the Sacred Green
Being thine, come forth let boasted scene,
The vast Atlantic spread between,
Can equal thee Kilkee-the -grand!

Let scented gales their treasures bear
O'er plumed Ceylon and bright Cashmere;
Be Cheli's peaks without compare;
To Como from Calabria fair.
No brilliant by Hesperian sea,
Nor Orient pearl, jewelled Italy,
Can dim the glow that lustres thee,
Ierna's gem, Kilkee-the-grand!

What time was wrecked that halcyon isle
Whose fall th' Egyptian told erstwhile,
(Whose vision still doth men beguile,
When Eve reflects that amaranth smile)
'Twas then was cleft thy sculptured coast,
Our Edward's empire's proudest boast,
Of thrilling plaudits worthy toast,
Atlanta's bride, Kilkee-the-grand!

M. A, MacNamara, *Kilkee-the-Grand,* (Galway, 1904)

The celebration of the beauty of the Edwardian watering-place caused many a
poetaster to burst into lyrical praise but few went the lengths of Miss Mac
Namara who composed anthem music to go with this celebration of the only
bourgeois seaside resort on the West Coast

The sea-bathing craze which, highly recommended by medical men 'for reasons of health', had swept England during the 1860's had an equal effect upon Irish resorts. The custom of wearing bathing costumes was a later and undesirable development as were such soft notions as Ladies bathing places. In Kilkee the ladies won hands down as one English visitor records: 'Wishing to bathe I ask a woman on the sand the regulations of the place. She said ladies might bathe from the machines, or boxes rather, at any time of the day they pleased but gentlemen only within particular hours, which had long passed. 'What', said I, 'not from a box?' 'No', she replied, 'not nohow.' This seems rather one-sided; however, nothing remains to be done but to walk over the hills to the north and to have an uncomfortable bathe from a recess under the rocks, for the sea was beating in strongly.'

An Englishman, *A Walking Tour Round Ireland in 1865* (London, 1867)

Below: *Kilkee Amphitheatre (Lawrence Collection, National Library)*

"Don't be comparing grandmother with lumps of children, like Patsy," said Jane Katy sharply. " 'Tis different altogether, and that's why I want to explain to you. Have you your copy-book below?"

"Yes, an' my pin-an'-ink," said Tommy eagerly. Jane Katy was a "good scholar," who had gone triumphantly through the Fourth Book and the double rule of three and wrote a beautiful "copperplate" roundhand. To get a copy set by Jane Katy, would be something, indeed.

"Very well," his cousin said. Bring 'em up with you in the morning. Are you out of the words with one syllable yet?"

"Yerrah, one syllable!" he said indignantly. "I could spell the longest of 'em as fast as I'd walk — b-l-a-s-t, blast; t-r-i-b-e, thribe; s-p-e-a-k, speak; — an' plenty more like that."

"Yes. Well, I'll give you a copy in your own book, and the same copy to grandmother in hers—a nice half-hard and half-easy one—'Strike the iron while 'tis hot,' or, maybe, 'Praise a fair day at night.' "

"Oh! wait till you'll see the way I'll write it," Tommy interrupted excitedly, "an' as fast as the wind—"

"But that's what I don't want you to do at all," said Jane Katy. "You must take plenty of time with it, for grandmother is always terrible careful and slow with her copies,—like any good scholar. You ought to understand, yourself, that good writing is better than—fast writing."

"I suppose it is," admitted Tommy, not wholeheartedly. "Well, I'll take time with it so!"

"And here's a Spelling Book Superseded, with some grand words of two syllables—"

"Oh, show 'em to me! Ut! Ut! I can spell an' pronounce everyone of 'em," cried Tommy. "Although, it may be I couldn't write 'em all right," he added conscientiously.

Julia Crottie, *Neighbours* (London, 1900)

Baltimore School, Co. Cork (Lawrence Collection, National Library)

JULIA CROTTIE was born in Lismore, Co. Waterford in 1853 but lived most of her life in the Isle of Man. Her best work is a series of realistic sketches of small town Irish life, which were published under the general title of *Neighbours.*

The *'Technical School of Fisheries'* was opened in Baltimore in 1848 with help from the Baroness Burdett Coutts. The founder was Fr. Davis to whom a memorial was erected in the grounds. Baltimore was an ideal situation for such an institute. Later under the agency of the Congested Districts Board a vessel called the *Saturn* was established as a floating laboratory. The mackerel fishery was protected by the *Helen*. The boom years before 1900 saw much shipping of cured mackerel to the US from this area.

Net-making at Baltimore School (Lawrence Collection National Library)

THIS EVENING A CIRCUS was advertised in Dingle, for one night only; so I made my way there towards the end of the afternoon, although the weather was windy and threatening. I reached the town an hour too soon, so I spent some time watching the wild-looking fishermen and fishwomen who stand about the quays. Then I wandered up and saw the evening train coming in with the usual number of gaily-dressed young women and half-drunken jobbers and merchants; and at last, about eight o'clock, I went to the circus field, just above the town, in a heavy splash of rain. The tent was set up in the middle of the field, and a little to the side of it a large crowd was struggling for tickets at one of the wheeled houses in which the acrobats live. I went round the tent in the hope of getting in by some easier means, and found a door in the canvas, where a man was calling out: 'Tickets, or money, this way,' and I passed in through a long winding passage.

The performance was begun by the usual dirty white horse, that was brought out and set to gallop round, with a gaudy horse-woman on his back, who jumped through a hoop and did the ordinary feats, the horse's hoofs splashing and possing all the time in the green slush of the ring. An old door-mat was laid down near the entrance for the performers, and as they came out in turn they wiped the mud from their feet before they got up on their horses. A little later the clown came out, to the great delight of the people. He was followed by some gymnasts, and then the horse-people came out again in different dress and make-up, and went through their old turns once more. After that there was prolonged fooling between the clown and the chief horseman, who made many mediaeval jokes, that reminded me of little circuses on the outer boulevards of Paris, and at last the horseman sang a song which won great applause:

Here's to the man who kisses his
    wife,
And kisses his wife alone;
For there's many a man kissed
    another man's wife
When he thought he kissed his
    own.

Here's to the man who rocks his
    child,
And rocks his child alone;
For there's many a man rocked
    another man's child
When he thought he rocked his
    own.

J. M. Synge, *In Wicklow and West Kerry* (Dublin, 1910)

The most obvious characteristic of Synge's work is his pleasure in wildness, of character, of imagination, of language and of life. As he wrote in the foreword to *The Playboy*: . . . 'the wildest sayings and ideas in this play are tame indeed, compared with the fancies one may hear in any little hillside cabin in Geesala, Carraroe, or Dingle Bay.' He sought this wildness in Wicklow, Kerry and Connemara. This description of a Dingle circus is typical of the passion and colour that he loved, in spite of a fastidiousness that he never lost. The faint embarrassment at the horesman's mildy bawdy song is one of several indications that the evangelicanism of the Co. Antrim Traills, inherited from his mother, was never totally exorcised.

Johnnie Patterson, well-known clown, and partner at circus at Deerpark, Co. Tipperary, 1890. (Mae Stallard/Carrick Society)

Chevalier O'Dowlam Thomas O'Brile, and Roland Glenpower remained loyal in their allegiance to Mr. Fireframe, and were, therefore, most abnoxious to the clerical party. The minds of the laity were confused. The Land Acts had failed to realise the sanguine expectations of the farmers, and the labourers were still struggling for new cottages. Legislation, it had been found, could not supply the want of regular industry in the community. Irish produce had lost its place in the British markets, where the Dane, the Norman, and the Colonial now carried off the lion's share of the profits. The people were in a remorseful frame of mind, suffering from a reaction after the undue excitement of the agitation, and were, therefore, plastic material for the religious experts to operate upon.

Under these circumstances the priests redoubled their efforts to concentrate upon themselves the attention of the uneducated masses; and ceremonial succeeded ceremonial, mission followed mission, in quick succession all over the diocese. Constant appeals for money were sent forth from the altars. Gallowglass new church, erected in Bullrush Street and now dominating the town, was dedicated with an amount of pomp and ritual which dazzled the barony of Killafastare.

There were present and officiating at the function the Cardinal himself, the Archbishop of Tara and Lough Neagh, and six bishops. The brass bands, which used to turn out for Mr. Fireframe and his political friends, now serenaded the Irish-Roman ecclesiastics in whose honour torchlight processions were arranged and public holidays were decreed. A religious pageant, in which the Host was carried under a canopy of cloth of gold by the Cardinal, marched through the Main Street. The "Prince of the Church," as the newspapers styled him, resplendent in his red hat and robes; the archbishop; the six bishops; the hundreds of priests of all ranks; the confraternities of surplices boys and little girls in white; the thousands of grown men, mostly labourers, with ribbons and medals suspended round their necks; all constituted a display of supernatural power by which those who beheld it felt overawed.

Father Lawnavawla rushed out of the procession and knocked Mr. McCameron's hat off his head, because the unimaginative Scotchman did not remove it when the Cardinal, bearing the Host, was passing the Distillery Road. The luxuries supplied from Canon O'Darrell's larder at the evening banquet eclipsed all the previous records of hospitality achieved at the Parochial House.

In fine, religion was rampant in Gallowglass, and, of all the townsfolk, the O'Dowlas and the O'Briles seemed to be the only people uninfected by the contagion of delirium. Both families stood aloof from the proceedings, and when they surveyed all the superstition and ritualism by which they were surrounded, the feeling uppermost in their minds was a thrill of disgust at such a debasement of Christianity to the level of fetichism. Even Mrs. O'Dowla, though she attended the devotions, has "lost the faith" so far as to abstain from spending any money on masses "for special intentions," or on the other religious indulgences in which there was such a colossal bosom.

It was when this fervour was at its height, shortly after the solemn dedication of Gallowglass new church, that the election of medical officer for the infirmary took place, and Ignatius O'Dowla was ignominiously defeated by the incompetent Doctor O'Grauver.

Michael J. F. MaCarthy, *Gallowglass*
(London, 1904)

MICHAEL J. F. McCARTHY was educated at Midleton College, Co. Cork and TCD and had a colourful career as anti-cleric. His book *Five Years in Ireland* (1901) is a list of crimes committed by church and clergy against the people. *Gallowglass* still in the same vein was a fictional satire which at times rises to heights of uproarious invective.

Monk outside Mt Melleray (Lawrence Stereoscopic Collection, National Library)

IN A FIELD, surrounded by a hedge, sat an old man. He appeared to be long past middle age, but still seemed hale and strong. His habiliments were extensively patched, said patches not always agreeing in colour. Around, under the hedge, were seated about fifty or sixty boys. Some of these had seats built of turf, constructed by themselves for their own special use and accommodation, and their exclusive right to which was never invaded by their schoolmates. The schoolmaster's seat—for such was the avocation of the individual we have already mentioned, and whose external adornment was completed by a leathern cap and a huge pair of horn spectacles—was, in its way, quite a pretentious affair, and was built of sods of turf welded by clay into a solid mass, and then overlaid with grass. There were also some attempts at decoration, which gave additional dignity and importance to the structure, both in the eyes of the builders themselves, who were some of the elder boys, and their friends.

The pupils, as we have said, were seated around the field under the hedge. The greater numbers were barefooted, some had no coats, and many were without coat or vest; but we question whether among the students of a fashionable academy there was more light-hearted, innocent gaiety or more genuine racy wit.

The schoolmaster, at the period of which we write, was seated in his chair of state hearing the lesson of a little boy, whose head did not indicate any very recent acquaintanceship with either comb or brush. In his right hand he grasped a cane symbol alike of his authority and power to compel obedience. The lesson he was engaged in hearing was grammar, and the pupil acquitted himself most creditably, and to the entire satisfaction of the master, as was evidenced by the expression of approval visible in the latter's countenance.

E R McAuliffe *Grace O'Donnell* (Dublin 1891)

The Industrial Schools were established under the *Habitual Criminals Act* of 1869 which incorporated the main provisions of the English *Industrial Schools Act* of 1861. The schools were meant to relieve 'the little sufferer and the community, without waiting until vice and crime shall have effaced all innocence and moral goodness.' In other words children could be sent there by a JP on such non-charges as begging, vagrancy, destitution and consorting with low company.

E R McAULIFFE was born in Cork in the early 19th-century and died in 1916. Her only recorded work is *Grace O'Donnell* (1891) an historical novel of Irish life in Penal Ireland with excellent period detail of the sufferings of catholics, and graphic accounts of hedge-schools, tithe-collectors and other horrors of subjugation.

ndustrial School, Cashel (Lawrence Collection National Libary)

JOHN. He must so. But he'd be more knowledgable still if he had a wife to teach him.

MALACHI. And more shame to you, John Fitzgibbon, to be saying the like and you knowing dam well the promise I made me mother.

T.J. And what was that, Malachi?

MALACHI. That I'd marry no gerril without herself consenting. Sure 'twas in terror she always was I'd take up with some common cauboge of a creature from the village, for I was always a soft man with the women, and so I promised her. And now God rest her, she's dead, and I'll go a single man to me grave.

JOHN. And is it spoiling the living you'll be, Malachi Phelan, for the sake of the dead?

MALACHI. 'Twas a great feeling I had for her, John, and sure I wouldn't go agen her for the world. 'Twould draw bad luck on me.

T.J. 'Twas the pity of God she went so sudden.

MALACHI. Aye so. Mixing food for the pigs she was, and she gave one screech, and after that the speech was whipped from her the way she never spoke after—

T.J. (crossing himself). Holy Virgin, but that was no Christian way to die.

JOHN. And do you mean to tell me you're going to live a puckered man on the hillside, because an old woman fell into her grave without speech?

MALACHI (with a wink). If I'm puckered I'm safe, John. Sure the promise is a great fence round the alatar, and God knows if I broke it maybe herself would come back to haunt me.

JOHN. If she came back to teach you sense, 'twould be the good work for her.

MALACHI. Maybe so. Women have great knowledge in affairs of love.

JOHN. They have so, there's Mary now. Begannies, meself would be glad of a word of advice about her. 'Tis time she settled down, but 'tisn't every man would please her.

MALACHI. Why wouldn't she take Timothy James there?

JOHN. Yerra, Mary wouldn't consort herself with the likes of him. It's a strong farmer with good land and an odd sheep or two she'll be looking for.

T.J. (ruffled by John's contempt). There's no fear she'll look at Malachi anyway. Sure she says he'd frighten maggots from a corpse.

JOHN. What the devil do you mean by saying that? It isn't likely she'd tell you what she thought of Malachi Phelan.

T.J. She tolt Katie Downey, anyway.

JOHN. Tcah. Katie Downey, that would give the skin off her feet to marry him herself.

MALACHI. I passed her now and I coming down the road. She's an on-coming woman is Katie. She has me that haunted, the flutter of a petticoat puts me in a palpitation.

JOHN. You'll have no peace till you marry. Be said by me now, choose a sensible wife and settle down with her on the hill above.

MALACHI. A sensible woman? And where do you suppose I'd find one?

JOHN. Maybe ye mightn't have to travel as far as you think.

MALACHI. If I travelled from here to the Equator I couldn't be matched with one of them. My cripes! but the female sex is hard to unravel.

T.J. You have no opinion of them at all, I'm thinking, Malachi.

MALACHI. I have not, and may the Saints themselves protect me from falling into their clutches.

(A plateful of wet tea leaves skilfully thrown through the doorway falls on Malachi, spattering and wetting him. He springs to his feet shaking himself.)

JOHN. Mary! Mary! What in the name of God are you doing?

MARY (thrusting an innocent face round the door). What ails ye, John?

G D Cummins & S Day, *Fox and Geese* (Dublin, 1917)

GERALDINE DOROTHY CUMMINS & SUZANNE DAY both born in Cork in 1890 collaborated on several Abbey plays including *Broken Faith* (1912) and *Fox and Geese* (1917). In later life Miss Cummins published a novel, *The Fires of Beltane* (1936) but is better known as the best Irish biographer of Edith Somerville. *Fox and Geese* has as theme the perennial tragi-comic situation of the ageing oedipal Irish bachelor considering the possibility of marriage.

Mountain Stage Cabin, Glenbeigh Co. Kerry (Lawrence Collection, National Library)

A 'stage' cabin was one in use during the summer months for 'booleying'—the practice traditional in Irish husbandry of moving with the cattle to mountain pastures.

27

Meadowvale Creamery, Charleville, Co. Cork (Lawrence Collection, National Library)

There was a loud call for the 'sets' from an impatient young man seated on the end of the table nearest the room-door. Thereupon a chair was placed in a convenient position for the concertina player, who, having fixed himself in it, commenced at playing the usual tune, his countenance assuming that half-comical, half-diabolical expression which seems inseparable from the endeavour of trying to knock sweet sounds out of the now very common, cheap German instruments.

The selection of partners was now about to take place, when all of a sudden frantic cries of joy and loud shouts of laughter arose in all directions. This was caused by a very unlooked-for movement on the part of Mr. Reilly, who, having bounded on to the middle of the floor, signified his intention to take part in the dance. Then, amidst much disconcerting applause, he advanced, with somewhat faltering footsteps to procure a partner. But when he got to where Katie Dolan and Johanna Ruane were chatting together, it would be easy for anybody who knew anything of his secret to observe that he was then in a state of intense nervousness. He stood before them for a second, his heart palpitating widly.

At last said he—"Will you dance with me, miss, if you plaze?'

Katie Dolan's soft orbs were raised for an instant, then fell with precipitation.

A shade of perplexity was visible on Johanna Ruane's broad-shining countenance.

In truth Philip's courage had pitfully vamoosed at 30 the critical moment; he was staring at an imaginary point in the wall parallel with Katie's pole. No wonder both the girls were in a dilemma!

The short but painful pause was broken by Johanna Ruane.

'Yerra, Phil's, she cried with a loud titter, Is it me or Katie you want?'

He withdrew his gaze from the wall in a twikling. At that moment the poor fellow felt overwhelmed with shame and a helpless kind of vexation.

"Sure amn't I after axin' ye, Johanna?' he said half-fiercely, but with such well-feigned astonishment at her doubting it, as it were, that that young damsel's mind became so confused as to baffle description. So Philip heroically carried her through the 'sets', whilst poor Katie Dolan sat strangely silent on the stool. But never did Phil Reilly go through the several parts of the dance so mechanically before—his body in motion but the dead weight almost of coma on his mind. No wonder that once or twice his partner found herself comparing him quite unfavourably with many of the other boys! and this in spite of the fact that he danced in his old graceful manner—that manner that had become a part of him almost. Indeed, when they had reached the sixth set—where everybody changes partners for each revolution till in the finish he winds up with his own—Johanna felt an obvious relief, for with Phil in his present incomprehensible mood she could by no means give herself up to that unbounded hilarity and abandon which usually ensues in the last part of the 'sets' in the Kingdom of Kerry.

George Fitzmaurice, *The Crows of Mephistopheles* (Dublin, 1970)

*Group assembled for cross-roads dance at Glenpatrick, Co.
Waterford slate-quarries c.1880. (Photograph Croke of Clonmel) (Hugh Ryan, Carrick Society)*

GEORGE FITZMAURICE was born in Listowel in 1877 and spent most of his deliberately obscured life as a minor civil servant in Dublin. He was one of the first playwrights to make his name in the early days of the Abbey and had a remarkable success with *The Country Dressmaker* in 1908. In all he wrote sixteen plays which were published after his death in three volumes representing the three main categories of his work, Folk, Fantasy and Realistic. Though he had claim to property and position in his native Kerry he preferred the anonymous life of the city clerk. *The Crows of Mephistopheles* is a collection of his short stories edited by Professor Robert Hogan. The excerpt is from 'The Bashfulness of Philip Reilly' which first appeared in *The Weekly Freeman* on 19 March 1904. He died in 1963.

32　*At Waterville, Co. Kerry (Lawrence Collection, National Library)*

City Town Country

For the purpose of getting into touch with my fellow-passengers I always carry with me newspapers of various kinds, and it is seldom that one of them does not give a starting point for a conversation. This afternoon I had *The Irish Times*, *The Leader* and *Grania*—the latter being an obscure little paper of very extreme views, which only lived for a year or two. I tried the young man first with *The Irish Times*.

He took his eyes from the fields and came back to current affairs with an obvious effort, and I had to repeat my offer. He thanked me, but said he had already read the paper.

He had a southern accent but not in any marked degree. In my mind I registered him as a gentleman by birth, and, probably a Protestant. To make sure I pressed the other two papers on him.

He looked at *Grania* first. I think he can never have seen the paper before (its circulation, indeed, was infinitesimal), it evidently puzzled him very much, but as soon as he caught the drift of it he allowed his mouth to smile a little—in faint pity, I suppose—and laid the paper gently on the seat. His father is a Unionist, I said to myself.

I knew that no young man of that age in Ireland coming up from the country for the first time (as I somehow guessed this young man was coming) has any political or religious views except those which he has inherited from his parents. I knew that in his native place Catholicism or Protestantism, Unionist or Home Ruler, cling to certain families like scent to flowers: a change in either is a thing monstrous and abnormal. But to make quite certain I watched his face as he read *The Leader*.

Really it was rather violent that week. I confess I felt a little ashamed of myself as I saw him reading it, a little ashamed of my fellow-Catholics who can support and enjoy such a paper, a little disgusted by its vulgarity.

Lennox Robinson, A Young Man from the South (Dublin, 1917)

LENNOX ROBINSON was born at Douglas, Cork in 1886 and educated at Bandon Grammar School. In spite of fervent nationalism caught in 1907 and never recovered from, he remained, as he wrote in The Bell (June 1944) 'a hopeless case from the catholic point of view.' As manager of

the Abbey Theatre in May 1910 he
decided not to close the theatre when
Edward VII died and thus helped
speed Miss Horniman on her way
back to Manchester for good. Author
of many plays including the hilarious
Drama At Inish he wrote only one
novel, **A Young Man from the South**
(1917). His contribution to the theatre
in Ireland is perhaps underrated. He
died in 1958.

Main Street, Bandon, Co. Cork (Lawrence Collection, National Library)

When Mr. Neville came to discuss the evidence for the footprints of his glacier in more detail, he found his lively companion less communicative; but a man once put in good humour with his own knowledge seldom objects to imparting more than he receives. Jack Harold know enough about geology, as about many other things, to be able to throw a certain lambent brightness over what he could not understand; and Mr. Neville informed Miss Westropp that they had had a most interesting chat, and that he found Gougaun Barra charming; upon which Mabel shot a glance of gratitude to our young geologist.

'But what on earth has become of our American Captain? I thought he was with you,' exclaimed Miss Westropp, in some alarm.

The Rector put his finger to his lips, and pointed to a figure half concealed by the ruined wall that overhung the Holy Well. They stole over on tiptoe and looled in. Captain Mike was on his knees bareheaded under the wild ash tree which shaded the Holy Well, and whose branches were drooping under the poor tags of coloured cloth which were hung there by grateful pilgrims. There was something in the spectacle of the bronzed soldier, kneeling there under the open sky, his hands clasped, and his great chest shaken with strong emotion, which caused the lookers-on to hold their breath, and the men unconsciously to doff their hats. The soldier rose, his bosom still heaving. He pulled out a large blue silk handkerchief, and drew it across his eyes; and then, as if a sudden thought had struck him, knotted the handkerchief to one of the boughs of the ash tree among the peasants' humble tributes of their faith. He knelt down again at the foot of the ash tree and pulled out his clasp-knife. The lookers-on watched him with painful intentness. He scooped out carefully with his knife a tiny green sod at the root of the wild ash, placed it tenderly in his hat, which he put on his head, and then rose to go. As he did so, and before they could retreat, his eye caught the guilty faces of the eaves-droppers. He was not in the least disconcerted.

'So, I guess you people seen the whole show?' he said, good humouredly. 'Wal, it does a man good to make a real stark blithering moon-calf of hisself once in a life or so, anyway. There is nothin' in our Re-publican Constitooshun agen it. No, sir! 'Tis three-and-twenty year last Lady Day in Harvest since I paid my rounds before at St.

Fin Barr's Well. There were them with me then that are not here now—that never'll be here again. God rest you, little Mauryeen, an' the poor ould father, Jack!'

'Amen,' said Father Phil reverently. 'He was a decent man!'

'I guess a petrified old Grand Army man's got things to sink Artesian wells in him when he looks back to his boyhood a few, and I just struck water there a moment ago, that's all. Don't you be skeered, Rector, at my hangin' up the han'kecher on that ould bush. When a man sheds a tear or two on bottom principles, over all that's past an' gone, I kind o' think an honest Irish saint will be as glad to get 'em as if they was di'monds the size of a Wall Street speculator's.'

Miss Westropp looked as if she could have kissed Captain Mike's gunpowder-stained yellow cheek.

'An the green sod you cut?' she whispered softly.

'Oh!' laughed Captain Mike, taking off his hat, and

Lady Day in Harvest since I paid my rounds before at St.

surveying its verdant contents complacently. 'Wal, you see, Missie, I couldn't get the saint's autograph lyin' around nohow, so I thought the next best thing would be a sprig of shamrock that was wathered with his blessin'. I've got an ould mother out yonder in East Thirty-second Street, Worcester, Mass, corner Kalabash Avenue, and won't her ould eyes jest skip when she sees that or'nery lookin' sod of Irish airth! Guess she'll go prayin' around a darn'd sight holier than if 'twar a block of real estate willed to the family—'twill fit where the real estate won't, in her coffin. An' you go Nap! she'll bring it along where she's goin'; and if I don't see them shamrocks shinin' in Heaven yet—wal, 'twill be because even the ould mother's prayers can't smuggle a perditioned old grizzly from the Ninth Massachusetts inside the line.'

William O'Brien, *When We Were Boys* (London, 1890)

WILLIAM O'BRIEN was born in Mallow in 1852. He became editor of Parnell's paper, *United Ireland* in 1881. His 'pepper-pot' style and flamboyant politics caused him to spend some time in jail, serving in all nine terms. Indeed he blamed the length of his famous book, *When We Were Boys* (1890) upon the length of his sentence, saying that if it had been shorter he could have been more economical in his verbal effects. The book is about the sentimental education of a Fenian and portrays with little disguise such real characters as Archbishop Croke and the author's brother, Jim. He died in 1928.

'In the middle of a scrubby grove, a little way from the en-closure, is a wishing-stone, which had evidently been much used, I hope to good purpose, for the stone itself was covered with trinkets and the bushes around were hung thickly with rags and hairpins and rosaries and other tokens. I picked up somewhere, perhaps from the jargon of the guide, that this wishing-stone is the altar of Fin Barre's old chapel, but I haven't been able to veryify this, and it may not be so; but the game is to put up a prayer to the saint, and make your wish, and leave some token to show that you are in earnest, and the wish will surely come true. Of course we made a wish and added some half-pennies to the collection on the altar. In turning over the trinkets already deposited there, we were amused to find two bright Lincoln cents.'
Burton E Stevenson, *The Charm of Ireland* (London, 1915)

St Finnbar's Oratory, Gougane Barra, Co. Cork (Lawrence Collection, National Library)

IT WAS AN APRIL morning in the Irish town of Waterford; beyond the suburbs, the grass lay thick and green upon the country-side in the virgin freshness of the spring, and the chestnuts glinted with the delicate sheen of bursting leaves; but in the streets, the dust of March was whirling to the April breeze, powdering the narrow by ways with a cloak of grey, eddying in a mad dance along the open spaces.

Portion of this dusty, characteristic, sparsely-populated town is dedicated to business—the business of the shops; a second and more important portion of it is given over to the quays, from whence a constant traffic is carried on with the hereditary enemy, England; while a third part, that holds itself aloof from commerce, is to be reckoned as half residential, half professional. It is to this third quarter that the eye of the story-seeker must turn on this April morning; for it is here, Lady Lane,—a thoroughfare as long and narrow as a Continental street, composed of tall old houses with square-paned windows and mysterious hall doors giving entry to vast and rambling interiors,—that the story, comedy or tragedy, is to find its stage; here, in the dining-room of one of the flat-fronted houses, that the student of human nature is to take his first glance at Stephen Carey—hero, so far as middle-class Irish life produces heroes, of the anticipated romance.

A man's room, one would have said at half a glance,—moreover, the room of a man self-made! There was no art, no beauty suggested or displayed; but there was comfort of a solid kind in the fire that burned ruddily in the grate, and in the breakfast-table that stood awaiting occupation. A man's room, although a closed work-basket stood on the sideboard, and the china on the table indicated breakfast for two.

And this first impression would have proved correct; for if the title of man be won by work, by patience, by a spirit that holds firm in face of great odds, then Carey's room was unquestionably the property of a man; for he had carved his own path to worldly success, hewing it from the rough material by days of toil and nights of thought.

Carey was a type,—a type of that middle class which by right of strength has formed its huge republic, and spread like a net over civilisation—invincible, indispensable as the vast machines from which it has sucked its power. It is as parent of this new republic that the nineteenth century will go down to futurity; and it is from the core of this new republic, virile in its ambition, tyrannical in its moral code, jealous of its hard-won supremacy, that we have garnered such men as Carey—the men of steel, drawn from the great workshops, tempered, filed, polished to fit the appointed place; helping to move the mighty engine of which they are the atoms, useless if cast out from its mechanism.

Katherine C. Thurston, *The Fly on the Wheel* (London, 1908)

KATHERINE CECIL THURSTON, nee Madden in Cork in 1875, was a firmly friend of Parnell and a nationalist. She married the 'anti-catholic' writer, E. Temple Thurston, in 1901 and published her first novel, *John Chilcote MP* in 1904. She divorced her husband in 1910 and committed suicide a year later. *The Fly on the Wheel* (1908) set in middle-class Waterford describes an unhappy love affair between a married man and a young girl who takes her own life.

Barron Strand Street, Waterford, 1901 (Lawrence Collection, National Library)

ROBERT DWYER JOYCE born in Glenosheen, Co. Limerick in 1830 was the younger brother of P. D. Joyce the Irish antiquarian and linguistic scholar whose *Old Celtic Romances* had such an effect upon Yeats and the other writers of the Anglo-Irish Renaissance. He lived in America for seventeen years where he had a successful and exclusive medical practice; it was there that he published most of his work: Prose, *Legends of the Wars in Ireland* (1868) and *Irish Fireside Tales* (1871) and verse, *Ballads of Irish Chivalry* (1872). To these should be added a collection published in Ireland in 1861., *Ballads, Romances and Songs.* The poem, *The Ballad of Dark Gilliemore,* is set in the Suir Valley, near the town of Carrick.

John Wogan of Castle Street, Carrick-on-Suir, solicitor and last seneschal of the Butlers. (Photograph taken April 1865 by McGrath of Carrick.) (Hugh Ryan/Carrick Society Collection)

A seneschal was the official in the house of a sovereign or great noble to whom the administration of justice and the entire control of domestic arrangements was entrusted.

I PLEDGE ye, comrades, in this cup
Of usquebaugh, bright brimming up;
And now while winds are blowing rude
Around our camp fire in the wood,
I'll tell my tale, yet sooth to say
It will be but a mournful lay.

Glenanner is a lovely sight,
Oun-Tarra's dells are fair and bright,
Sweet are the flowers of Lisnamar,
And gay the glynns 'neath huge Benn Gar;
But still, where'er our banner leads,
'Mid tall brown hills or lowland meads,
By storied dale or mossy down,
My heart goes back to Carrick town.

By Carrick town a castle brave
Towers high above its river wave,
Well belted round by wall and fosse
That foot of foe ne'er strode across.

Well belted round by wall and fosse
That foot of foe ne'er strode across.
Look on me now—a man am I
    Of mournful thoughts and bearing sad;
Yet once my hopes flowed fair and high,
    And once a merry heart I had;
For I was squire to Ormond then,
    First in his train each jovial morn
He flew his hawks by moor and fen,
Or chased the stag by rock and glen
    With music sweet of hound and horn.
Young Ormond was a goodly lord
As ever sat at head of board.
If Europe's kings, some festal day,
Sat round the board in revel gay,
And he were there, and I in hall,
The seneschal to place them all,
I'd place him without pause or fault
Among their best above the salt.
You need not smile, Sir Hugh le Poer,
    Nor you, young Donal of Killare;
I'prove my words, ay, o'er and o'er,
    With skian   in hand and bosom bare,
Or sword to sword and jack to jack,
For sake of Thomas Oge the Black!

R. D. Joyce, 'The Ballad of Dark Gilliemore' from *Ballads of Irish Chivalry* (Boston, 1872)

41

Bridge Street, Skibbereen, Co. Cork (Lawrence Collection, National Library)

MY PRISON CHAMBER

My prison chamber now is iron lined,
An iron closet and an iron blind.
But bars, and bolts, and chains can never bind
To tyrant's will the freedom-loving mind.

Beneath the tyrant's heel we may be trod,
We may be scourged beneath the tyrant's rod,
But tyranny can never ride rough-shod
O'er the immortal spirit-work of God.

And England's Bible tyrants are, O Lord!
Of any tyrants out the cruelest horde,
Who'll chain their Scriptures to a fixture board
Before a victim starved, and lashed, and gored. . .

Without a bed or board on which to lie,
Without a drink of water if I'm dry,
Without a ray of light to strike the eye,
But all one vacant, dreary, dismal sky.

The bolts are drawn, the drowsy hinges creak,
The doors are groaning, and the side walls shake,
The light darts in, the day begins to break,
Ho, prisoner! from your dungeon dreams awake. . .

"Rossa, salute the Governor," cries one,
The Governor cries out—"Come on, come on,"
My tomb is closed, I'm happy they are gone,
Well—as happy as I ever feel alone.

J. O'Donovan Rossa, 'My Prison Chamber' in *Irish Literature VIII* (Philadelphia, 1904)

JEREMIAH O'DONOVAN *(ROSSA)* was born in Rosscarbery, Co. Cork in 1831. He first attracted the attention of the authorities when as a grocer in the town of Skibbereen he founded the literary and political group, the *Phoenix Society.* This was swept into the Fenian movement and O'Donovan remained a relentless Fenian for the rest of his life. His inevitable privations in English jails were described in *Prison Life* (1874). Exiled on amnesty in 1874 he went to America where he died in 1915. The arrival of his remains in Dublin were the occasion of one of Pearse's more emotional speeches: 'Life springs from death and from the graves of patriot men and women spring living nations' and the demonstration became the prototype of 44 many such in subsequent years.

Main Street, Lismore, Co. Waterford (Lawrence Collection, National Library)

The meeting of the waters between
Long Range and the middle lake,
Killarney, looking up towards Dinis
Cottage. (Lawrence Stereoscopic
Collection, National Library)

Nuair do bhúail an bheirt Cill Áirne b'eigean doibh deoch bheith aca i dtigh Shéamuis Ui Bhruighin 'sa Sráid Nuaidh, agus níor bh'fhada dhoibh go raibh braon eile aca i Sráid na gCearc nuair casadh orra nuair bhí an gabha súgach go leor.

Ní raibh Neilli i bhfad ar a' sráid gur chonnaic sí a hathair agus é ar leath-mheisge. Is gairid do bhí sí féin agus an cailín eile ag déanamh a ngnótha. Nuair do bhíodar ullamh chun teacht abhaile do dhein Neilli a dícheall a hathair do mhealladh leí, acht na raibh maitheas dí bheith a tathant air; d'fhan sé fein agus Séamuis ar an sráid go dti tuitim na hoídhche agus go rabhadar araon ar meisge nó i ngiorracht dó.

Bhí capaillín beag cneasta ag Séamus Táilliura. Bhí an bóthar reidh agus an oídhche geal, agus dá mbéadh an beirt sásta leis an méid do bhí ólta aca nuair fhágadar sráid Cill Áirne bhéadh an sgéal go maith aca, acht ní rabhadar. Nuair thángadar go Droichead na Leamhna bhi deoch le bheith aca, agus nuair bhí an gabha ag teacht amach as an dtrucaill thuit se ar fhleasg a dhroma ar an mbóthar, agus 'san am cheadna do chuir rud eigin an capall ar siubhal. Chuaidh an roth treasna láimhe Thaidhg. Do sgread an fear bocht cómh géar sin gur rith na daoine amach chuige, agus nuair chonnacadar e sínte ar an mbóthar shaoileadar go raibh a lámh briste, acht ni raibh.

Ba mhór an ní go raibh an dochtúir 'n-a chomhnaidhe ar thaoibh an bhóthair ag Droichidín na Spiodóige; bhí sé ag baile. Tar éis féachaint ar láimh an ghabha 'sé dubhairt an dochtúir, "Níl aon chnámh briste, acht beidh sé tamall go mbeidh greidhm agat ar chasúr, a Thaidhg."

Séamus Ó Dúbhghaill, *Tadhg Gabha* (Dublin, 1900)

SÉAMUS Ó DÚBHGHAILL was born in Tuogh, Co. Kerry in 1855. An excise officer he had postings all over the British Isles and was stationed in Derry at the height of his literary fame, which coincided with the years of greatest success of the Gaelic League (from 1898 to 1904). His first public appearance as a writer was at the second Oireachtas (1898)when he won a prize for three humorous stories in Irish. He was a regular prizewinner after this writing not only stories but phrase-books, grammars and general text-books. These last gave him a great if impish delight since he was not a teacher. Known in later life by the pseudonym *Beirt Fhear* from his book *Beirt Fhear o'n dTuaith* his best known work *Tadhg Gabha* became an examination textbook for those who wished to be travelling teachers. The piece describes an occupational hazard of the smith's life, aggravated by the plenitude of public houses in Killarney.

'The town of Killarney is next in importance to Tralee, the capital of the county, and it has a population of 5,204. It is situated about a mile to the eastward of the largest of the lakes, and consists of four streets of which the Main Street is the principal. There are many small streets and lanes inhabited by poor people, and the whole town looks miserably decayed, presenting a melancholy contrast to the rich landscapes that surround it. The demesnes of the gentry take up all the ground up to the town, not leaving room even for small gardens, where the people might cultivate some vegetables, and they complain much of the want of a supply of milk.'

J. Godkin & J. Walker, *Handbook of Ireland* (Dublin, c.1870)

College Street, Killarney (Lawrence Collection, National Library)

Picnic at Killarney (Lawrence Collection, National Library)

Puck Fair, Killorglin, Co. Kerry (Lawrence Collection, National Library

"Oh, glory be to goodness, Father, 'tis a yaller Munster top!" he croaked.

He became silent, put his head upon one side, with a look almost of antique coquetry, and regarded Father Egan with imperative beseeching.

"Oh, it's to whip it, is it?" Father Egan said. "And what'll I do for the whip!"

An eager snuffle sounding close at hand, Father Egan turned, to behold young Feeney sprung up in silent magic at his side, flicking his pinafore with a rag fastened to a stick, while he clenched the fingers of the other hand on some pet jewel of his play. The Priest took the stick with the rag-lash from the child; he chose the smoothest flagstone before the door of the house, gave a sharp twist of his two hands, and round the Munster top went spinning, so fast, you could not see it move.

The old man shut his eyes in rapture, and his mind went back to the scenes from which the Munster top had hailed.

"Oh, 'tis the third day of the Munster Fair!" he said, "the day the horses do be coming with the long tails floating to the town . . . and the little donkeys goin', and the littles asseens trottin' under them, and the foxy-haired Tinkers drivin' 'em in the dreepin' rain!" . . .

He opened his eyes to see Father Egan encouraging the Munster top.

"Would you ketch it in the hand!" he cried.

By this time a shawled group of women had gathered round the gate. For all the world as if they had never set their eyes upon a top before, they clapped their hands with glittering eyes, and spurred its whirling movements with cries of approbation, as though it were a greyhound at a coursing match. " 'Tis down!" cried one. " 'Tis goin' still!" cried another. "You could ate your dinner while 'twas dancin'!" cried a third.

Drawn to her own gate from a neighbour's house by cries, Sara Feeney now ran forth and joined the group.

"Glory be!" she cried, "if the darlin' man hasn't sent to Munster for the top!"

Rosamond Langbridge, *The Green Banks of Shannon* (London, 1929)

ROSAMOND LANGBRIDGE was born in Glenalla, Co. Donegal in 1880 but was brought up and educated in Limerick where her father was Rector of St. John's. An unspecific and quasi-mystical nationalist she regarded Ireland as 'the child-soul among nations' which put the 'Traffic of the Heart before the Traffic of the Mart'. The characters of her novels though pretty mild by our standards were regarded as a trifle 'fast' by the readers of her heyday. Her last book, *The Green Banks of Shannon* (1929) is a collection of pleasantly senti-mental sketches of life as she rem-embered it in her adopted county.

Puck Fair—Aonach an Phuic ('the fair of the he-goat) is held each year on the three days August 10—12 in the town of Killorglin, between Tralee and Cahir-civeen. The origins of the ritual are shrouded in mystery but the anthropological aspects of the goat and the revelry seems fairly obvious. The goat is hoisted on top of a platform in the market square on the evening of the first day (the 'gathering') and presides over the trafficking in cattle sheep and horses until the evening of the third day (the 'scattering'). The photograph shows the 'gathering' day; the *puc* not yet in position and a general air of restraint and respectability that tends to disappear as the fair gets in its stride. The streamer bearing in Irish the slogan, 'Victory and Strength to the united Gaelic League' places the scene as around 1898.

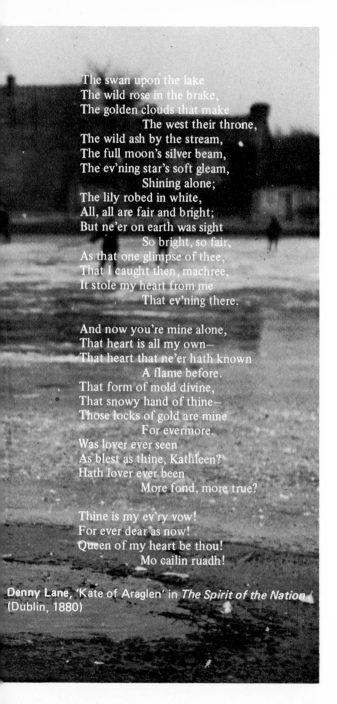

The swan upon the lake
The wild rose in the brake,
The golden clouds that make
      The west their throne,
The wild ash by the stream,
The full moon's silver beam,
The ev'ning star's soft gleam,
      Shining alone;
The lily robed in white,
All, all are fair and bright;
But ne'er on earth was sight
      So bright, so fair,
As that one glimpse of thee,
That I caught then, machree,
It stole my heart from me
      That ev'ning there.

And now you're mine alone,
That heart is all my own—
That heart that ne'er hath known
      A flame before.
That form of mold divine,
That snowy hand of thine—
Those locks of gold are mine
      For evermore.
Was lover ever seen
As blest as thine, Kathleen?
Hath lover ever been
      More fond, more true?

Thine is my ev'ry vow!
For ever dear as now!
Queen of my heart be thou!
      Mo cailin ruadh!

Denny Lane, 'Kate of Araglen' in *The Spirit of the Nation*
(Dublin, 1880)

DENNY LANE was born in Cork in 1818, the only child of Maurice Lane, a distillery owner. He is remembered for two poems 'Kate of Araglen' and 'An Irish Maiden's Lament' both of which appeared in *The Nation.* He was an ardent but sensible Young Irelander and warned the gorgeous peacocks of the Eighty-Two Club not to attempt to introduce their club uniform (like Robert Emmet's only more splendid in gold, green and white) into Cork because of the hatred of those citizens for uniform. 'This' he wrote in *The Nation,* I think, arises from the morbidly keen sense of the ludicrous that Cork men generally possess.' He died in 1899 having in his time been President of the Institute of Gas Engineers of Gt. Britain.

As they crossed the Norgate five times over,
  "The devil," says Padna, "Such light!"
Dinny Lucy clung on like a lover
  To Padna, "Begob 'tis a fright."

And they paused where the lamps on the water
  Danced up in reflections of red;
"Be the holy," says Din, "There's been
    slaughter—
Such blood!" "Yerra, God help your head!"

Padna pulled at his arm, reassuring,
  "Them lights are the lights on the port
Of grand ships with the cargoes maturing:
  'Tis bagging that lot 'll be sport."

But my Padna all through, and he straying,
  Watched out, "Oh we've passed Mallow
    Lane!"
"Yerra whisht," says Din Lucy, surveying,
  "We're down at the Jetties again."

So they clutched for a stanchion to steady
  The street that spun round like a midge,
An' Din dreaming cried, "Heave away, ready!"
  Till Padna said "Look! Vincent's Bridge!"

"Where the h–?" at that instant, such clatter
  And, rushing up, oh, I declare,
Katie Drew, (Padna's "flame"), an' no hat or
  Coat on her, and she "in a tear!"

An' "Come on!" and "Have sense!" and
  "Ye foolahs!"
Half coaxing—a woman knows how,—
"Christmas times," Padna whispered as cool as
  You please, Dinny dumb as a cow!

D. L. Kelleher, *Cork's Own Town* (Dublin, 1920)

DANIEL LAWRENCE KELLEHER was born in Cork in 1893 and set most of his poems in that city. *Cork's Own Town* is a ballad sequence in which the colour and vitality of 'the highly individualistic Southern City' is conveyed in the adventures and opinions of Padna Dee, the Cork 'cockney' born within the sound of Shandon Bells.

P.S. Albert on her regular service run to Queenstown, Crosshaven, Ringaskiddy and other wharfs on Cork Harbour. 1912. (Cork Examiner Collection)
The Albert, a 54-tonner plied, the Lee and Cork Harbour right up until 1925 when the steamers were withdrawn.

Excursion Crowd on Cork Quay with P. S. Albert dressed over all for excursion 1897 (Cork Examiner Collection).

Hospital Flag Day, Cork. c.1900 (Cork Examiner Collection)

"JURRY Jurry! Yerra, look, man alive!"

"What! Where? Yerra, what ails yi at all?"

"Look hether at Oul' Dan, th' oul' dickens! Look at what he's carryin' home to dround the Shamrock wid!"

It was at the Cork Terminus of the Muskerry Line on St. Patrick's Eve, and crowds of homeward-bound passengers were eagerly endeavouring to collect the parcels sent to meet them from the various shops.

As usual, pandemonium reigned supreme. A babel of messengers shouted at the tip top of their discordant voices the names of the firms they represented—"Cash-ays," "Bay-less," "Queen's Oul' Castle," "D'Arcade," &c., &c.— while the anxious passengers strained their ears to catch the name of the firm they were awaiting.

You thought you heard "D'Arcade" half way up the platform, and you elbowed through a packed crowd of equally anxious inquirers towards your goal, but when you reached it, as you thought, "D'Arcade" was being called "away back" where you started from! No messenger was ever known to remain in the same spot for five seconds; they dodge about up and down while the perplexed passengers follow the voices, as elusive as a score of corncrakes, hither and thither, and after endless elbowing catch the object of their hunt.

"Hallo, boy! are ye Bailey's?"

"Yes, Mistero!" finger touches cap politely.

Your name may be Buckley, Bung, or Blennerhassett, but it's "alldesame" to the messenger, the familiar "Mr. O" embraces the lot. He addresses you with the ease and intimacy of an old acquaintance.

"What name, Mistero?" he promptly inquires. You tell him, and he searches through his basket, and lifts up your parcel with much unnecessary exertion, and hands it over, looking anxiously into your eyes, canvassing the chances of a tip. If you are oblivious to his suggestive glances, several gentle hints are thrown out.

"Put it in di van for yi, Mistero?"

And he does so if you permit him, then comes back again, touching his cap profusely, assuring you—"Dass all right now, Mistero." And if you are still slow to respond he lingers on till his magnetic eyes draw coppers from even the most miserly!

"Oul' Dan" had come in to Cork to get the necessaries to celebrate St. Patrick's Day according to his own idea. The receipt of an unexpected twelve dollars from his daughter in New York helped him to prepare, and so he was well laden when Jack Fitz and Jurry Hegarty, two neighbouring lads, saw him at the station.

"A jar of whishkey, no less! Glory be to oul' Cork!" cried Jurry in surprise.

"Yes, man alive! and a basket of full aitables besides!" added Fitz.

"Ha, then," said Jurry reflectively. " 'tis he ought be sick wid the whishkey—'twas it losht the farm for him!"

"True for yi! All the same," added Fitz, "he's the dacint oul' Dan if he's fond o' the dhrop inself."

"Come over and we'll give him a hand," said Jurry.

The messenger boy was palavering oul" Dan for a tip.

"Dass all now, Mistero; de're all in," but Dan was dense.

"Ah, Mistero," persuasively urged the lad, "don't forget me Patrick's Pot, alldesame!"

At last oul' Dan was softened. After much cogitation he dug his hand deep down into his trousers something to the eagerly watchful boy, with a "Run away now and don't be botherin' me."

"Tanks! Tanks, Mistero!" Then finding his tip was only a single solitary copper, he wheeled round to a group of his colleagues, and holding the penny aloft between his fingers, remarked solemnly—"A box at di Palace Monday night!"

"Sound man, Dan!" said Fitz, patting the old fellow patronisingly on the back.

Oul' Dan looked around suspiciously and clutched his jar tightly.

"Oh, Jackey! is that you, a vic o? It's the dickens own—own job gettin' the parcels"—he was out of breath.

"Yer well loaded, Dan," said Fitz, smiling.

"Fairly. The little girl didn't forget me, God bless her! She sint me three poun'."

"Begor we'll be all callin' to see you to-night," said Fitz.

"An' welcome," said Dan, cheerfully.

William Cronin ('Liam), *A Hamper of Humour* (Dublin, 1913).

'LIAM' (WILLIAM CRONIN) was the author of a collection of sketches called *A Hamper of Humour* (1913) showing two interests that are almost obsessions, the Cork accent and trains.

Tram at Father Mathew Statue, Cork (1900) (Lawrence Collection, National Library)

Right: 'Irish Colleen' (Lawrence Collection, National Library)

A photograph taken almost certainly in Adare about 1898. It is very obviously posed, the girl if 'colleen' she be is wearing her Sunday best and perched precariously and temporarily upon a wooden cask.

GLAUCE

I love you, pretty maid, for you are younger:
I love you, pretty maid, for you are fair:
I love you, pretty maid, for you love me.

They tell me that, a babe, smiling you gazed
Upon the stars, with open, asking eyes,
And tremulous lips apart. Everlong, self-taught,
You found for every star and every flower
Legends and names and fables sweet and new.
I, since I loved you, am grown half immortal.

O that when far away I still might see thee!
How oft when wearied with the din of life
On thee mine eyes would rest, thy Latmian heavens
Brightening that orbed brow and those white shoulders!
Hesper should shine upon thee—lamp of Love,

Beneath whose radiance thou wert born.—O Hesper!
Thee will I love and reverence evermore.—
Bind up that shining hair into a knot,
and let me see that polished neck of thine
Uprising from the bed snow-soft snow-white
In which it rests so gracefully! What God
Hath drawn upon thy forehead's ivory plane
Those two clear streaks of sweet and glistening black
Lifted in earnest mirth or lovely awe?
Open those Peiad eyes, liquid and tender,
And let me lose myself among their depths!
Caress me with thine infant hands, and tell me
Old tales divine that love makes ever new
Of Gods and men entoiled in flowery nets,
Of heroes sighing all their youth away,
And which the fairest flower of Venus' isle.
Come forth, dear maid, the day is calm and cool,

58

And bright though sunless. Like a long green scarf,
The tall Pines crowning yon gray promontory
In distant ether hang, and cut the sea.
But lovers better love the dell, for there
Each is the other's world—How indolently
The tops of those pale poplars bending sway
Over the violet-braided river brim!
Whence comes their motion, for no wind is heard,
And the long grasses move not, nor the reeds?
Here we will sit, and watch the rushes lean
Like locks, along the leaden-coloured stream
Far off; and thou, O child, shalt talk to me
Of Naiads and their loves. A blissful life
They lead, who live beneath the flowing waters:
They cherish calm, and think the sea-weeds fair;
They love to sleek their tresses in the sun;
They love each other's beauty; love to stand
Among the lillies, holding back their tresses
And listening, with their gentle cheek reclined
Upon the flood, to some sweet melody
Of Pan or shepherd piping in lone woods,
Until the unconscious tears run down their face.
Mild are their loves, nor burdensome their thoughts—
And would that such a life were mine and thine!

    Aubrey de Vere, 'Glauce' from *Irish Odes and Other*
Poems (New York, 1869)

AUBREY DE VERE, was born in 1814 in Curragh Chase,
the ancestral home of the de Vere family, situated six miles
south east of Adare, Co. Limerick. The son of Sir Aubrey
de Vere (himself a poet) he was a romantic unionist.
Educated at Trinity he became a catholic in 1851 and an
obvious choice for the faculty of Newman's Catholic
University (though as Professor of Political and Social
Science) when that unique venture was established after
1852. Though his poetic works run as with most 19th-
century versifiers into many volumes his most successful,
and to modern taste most readable, work was *Inishfail,
A Lyrical Chronicle of Ireland* (1863). 'Glauce' is typical
of his bland and, considering his experience of women,
naive style. There is no suggestion in this mild ode that
the mythological Glauce was the woman that Jason rejected for Medea or that she died horribly at the hands
of that resourceful sorceress. He died unmarried in 1902.

*Adare, Co Limerick was the invention of the 3rd Earl of
Dunraven who had become a catholic at the time of the
Oxford Movement. Its exotic appearance, like a Costwold
village, was due to his interest in architecture and land-
scaping.*

*Broad Street, Adare, Co. Limerick (Lawrence Collection,
National Library)*

Scríobhas go mionchruinn ar a lán dár gcúrsai d'fhonn go mbéadh cuimhne i bpoll éigin orthu agus thugas íarracht ar mheon na ndaoine a bhí i mo thimpeall a chur síos chun go mbeadh a dtuairisc inár ndiaidh, mar ná beidh ar leithéidí arís ann.

Táim críonna anois. Is dócha gur iomdha rud eile a tháinig trasna orm i rith mo mharthan go dtí seo dá mbéadh slí sa cheann doibh. Tháinig daoine ar an saol le mo linn i mo thimpeall, agus d'imíodar. Níl ach cuigear is sine ná mé beo ar an oileán. Táid sin ar an mbunchíos; níl uaimse ach cupla mí, leis chun an dáit chéanna, dát nach rogha liom. Is ag bagairt chun báis a bhíonn sé, dar liom cé go bhfuil morchuid daoine arbh fhearr leó a bheith críonna agus an pinsean acu ná a bheith óg á éagmais, lucht na sainte agus an scanraidh.

Is cuimhin liom a bheith ar bhrollach mo mháthar. Thugadh sí suas ar an gcnoc mé i gclíabh a bhíodh ag tarraingt mhóna aici. Nuair a bhíodh an chlíabh lán den mhóin is faoina hascaill a bhínn ag teacht aici. Is cuimhin liom a bheith i mo gharsún; i m'fhear óg; i mbláth mo mhaitheasa agus mo nirt. Thainig gorta agus flúirse, ráth agus míráth le mo mharthain go dtí seo. Is mór an fhoghlaim a thugaid sin ar an nduine a thugann faoi ndeara íad.

Beidh an Blascaed lá gan aoinne den dream atá luaite agam sa leabhar seo—ná aoinne a mbeidh cuimhne aige orainn. Tugaim buíochas le Dia thug caoi dom gan an méid den saol a chonac féin agus a raghas ag broic leis a dhul amú, agus go mbeidh a fhios i mo dhiaidh conas mar a bhí an saol le mo linn agus na comharsain a bhí suas le mo linn agus an méid ata fós beo acu, gan focal searbh idir mé agus íad ríamh.

Rud eile, níl tír ná dúthaigh ná náisiún ná go dtugann duine an chraobh leis thar chách eile. Ó lasadh an chéad tine san oileán seo níor scríobh aoinne a bheatha ná a shaol ann. Fágann sin an chraobh ag an té a dhein é. 'Neosfaidh an scríbhinn seo conas mar a bhí na hoileánaigh ag déanamh sa tseanaimsir. Bhí mo mháthair ag tarraingt na móna agus mise ocht mbliana déag d'aois ar scoil aici. Tá súil le Dia agam go bhfaighidh sí fein agus m'athair an Ríocht Bheannaithe agus go mbuailfeadsa agus gach n-aon a léifidh an leabhar seo leó in Oileán Párthais.

Tomás Ó Criomhthain, *An tOileanach* (Ath Cliath, 1929)

TOMÁS Ó CRIOMHTHAIN (1856-1937) was born, lived and died on the Great Blasket Island off the coast of Co. Kerry, the greatest of the Irish writers who came from that area so incredibly fertile of writers. *An tOiléanach* is his life-story, written in a style so spare and muscular as almost to defy the skill of the translator and to deprive Europe of one of its finest pieces of primitive writing. Ó Criomhthain writes consciously of a vanishing way of life; as he notes with a kind of desperate pride: *mar beidh ár leithéidí aris ann.*

Tomás Ó Criomhthain at the door of his house, Great Blasket Island, Co. Kerry, 1932. (MacMonagle Collection)

61

At half-past one the town was silent,
Except a row raised in the Island,
Where Thady,—foe to sober thinking,—
With comrade lads, sat gaily drinking.
A table and a pack of cards
Stood in the midst of four blackguards,
Who, with the bumper-draught elated,
Dash'd down their trumps, and swore, and cheated.
Four pints, the fruits of their last game,
White-foaming, to the table came;
They drank, and dealt the cards about,
And Thady brought *fifteen wheel out.*
Again, the deal was Jack Fitzsimon's,
He turned them up, and trumps were diamonds;
The ace was laid, by Billy Mara,
And beat with five, by Tom O'Hara;
The queen was quickly laid, by Thady,
Jack threw the king, and douced the lady.
Bill jink'd the game, and cried out, "Waiter,
Bring in the round, before 'tis later!"
The draughts came foaming from the barrel;
The sport soon ended in a quarrel;—
Jack flung a pint at Tom O'Hara,
And Thady levell'd Billy Mara;
The cards flew round in every quarter,
The earthen floor was drunk with porter;
The landlord ran to call the Watch,
With oaths half English, and half Scotch.
The Watch came to the scene of battle,
Proclaiming peace, with sounding wattle;
The combatants were soon arrested,
But Thady got off unmolested.

Michael Hogan, 'Drunken Thady' from *Lays and Legends of Thomond* (Limerick, 1865)

O'Connell Street, looking towards Patrick Street, Limerick c.1870 (Lawrence Stereoscopic Collection, National Library).

MICHAEL HOGAN, known to many loyal hearts as 'The Bard of Thomond', was born in Limerick in 1832 and as a wheelwright, lampooner, broadsheet poet and nightwatchman lived a life more appropriate to 18th-century Grub Street than 19th-century Limerick. His main work, *Lays and Legends of Thomond,* is rather decorous compared with some of his satirical squibs. His invention, 'Drunken Thady' is fit to take his place beside Burn's 'Tam-o'—Shanter' in the hall of inebriate fame. The bard died in 1899.

Troubles

Cork Fire 1900 (Cork Examiner) 63

He pulled strongly, and woke to life a venerable old seaman, who was sleeping calmly in the shelter of the boats. He rose lazily, lazily drew himself together, and stared at the intruders.

"Hello, old salt," said Ashley, "we disturbed you! Is there any place in this Sleepy Hollow where we could get a bite, or a drink for our nags?"

James Carroll resented this familiarity for two reasons. First, because "old salt" was an irreverent expression to a man who had spent half his life before the mast in Her Majesty's Navy, and had several medals hanging up near the altar of the Blessed Virgin in his little bedroom at home. And second, because "Sleepy Hollow" was an untoward epithet for the cleanest, tidiest, healthiest little fishing hamlet in Ireland. He took up in silence the tar-brush with which he was coating the little fishing smacks that, with their broad, black blacks were now glistening in the hot sun, and, after a few moments' reflection, during which he was gathering his thoughts and concentrating them in a deadly form, he sent forth the missile.

"I'd give you one advice, young man, and maybe you'd thank me for it when you have grey hairs. There are two things that carry a man safe through life – the Grace of God, an' a civil tongue."

He bent down to his work again; but after a moment he thought he could improve on the aphorism.

"An' a civil tongue is no load," he said.

Ashley looked at his companion and laughed.

"Stranded, by Jove!" said he.

Hugh Ireton, more diplomatic, because more kind, said nothing; but running his horse's bridle under his arm, he took out his tobacco pouch and filled his pipe. Then, without offering it to Ashley, he said to the old mariner:—

"You have got your cutty about you?"

The old man hesitated for a moment between wounded pride and the temptation. But it was only for a moment. The flesh conquered the spirit; and, like most mortals, he yielded. He put his pride in his pocket and took out his pipe. He filled it well from the proffered pouch, and taking a light from the young man, he sat and smoked leisurely. When his anger, excited by the young man's ir-

reverence, had calmed down, he said apologetically:-

"Ye'll pardon me, young gintlemin, for the liberty; but we, old navy men, were always addressed respectful-like by our officers. And they had to mind their P's and Q's themselves, I tell ye. If the Lieutenant on watch had only to tell the Cap'n that the cook was drunk, he had to tech his cap and say:— 'I've the 'anner to report the cook is drunk, Sir!' and if the Cap'n replied:—'You may go to the devil, Sir!' the lieutenant had to tech his cap again, 'and say, respectful-like:—'Ay, ay, Sir!' That was manners for you. But this is rare tobacco!"

"May I be permitted, Sir, to join the pow-wow, Sir, with this?" said Ashley, holding out a capacious flask.

"Ay, ay, Sir," said Ireton. "But that's new whiskey, Ashley. Is there any fresh water around here?" he asked, addressing the old man.

"Ay, ay, Sir" said the latter, entering into the fun with twinkling eyes, and the expectation of better things.

He took them up to his little cottage; and a very neat, clean, well-kept cottage it was. For its tutelar deity was Anstie, James Carroll's only daughter, "the light of his life and the pulse of his heart.'. It was her pretty presence threw sunshine wherever she cast a shadow; and it was her swift, deft fingers that made the whole place a "moral" of neatness and beauty. Of course it was only a sailor's cabin; but the sailor's lass kept it as sweet as the stateroom in a British man-of-war.

Canon Sheehan, *Miriam Lucas,* (London, 1912)

PATRICK AUGUSTINE SHEEHAN was born in Mallow in 1852 and became parish priest of Doneraile in 1895. His tastes were scholarly and he was rather better read than most of his compeers—facts which influenced his literary style. His works have always been officially approved reading for the young and this has led to an unjust disregard and underrating. His portraits of priests, horn beads and all, have rarely been equalled; only in the work of Gerald O'Donovan is there comparable portraiture. Known to many who have never read the book as the author of *My New Curate* (1899) he wrote in all eleven novels of which *Luke Delmege* (1901) is probably the best. He became a DD in 1903 and died ten years later still pastor of Doneraile.

British Warship, 'Dreadnought' Class, Bantry Bay, 1907. (Lawrence Collection National Library)

The first of the class, HMS *Dreadnought* was launched in 1906, of 17900 tons and with a main armament of ten 12-in guns in five turrets and a speed of 22 knots. The gun turret may be seen centre picture with tompions covering the barrels. Bantry Bay was a good deep anchorage but somewhat unsheltered.

"A select combination of the circus and music-hall. I hope our 'umble endeavours will be acceptable to you—in fact, I—"

"No, sir, a penny is no good; fetch another one."

"In fact, I make no doubt you will be pleased that not only will you come back again to-morrow night, but that you will also bring those among you who have not come."

"One penny—half-price for the child, madam; our invariable rule."

"The performance will now open with the good old Punch and Judy Show, after which there will be variety entertainment, concluding with the wonderful magicograph, depicting scenes, sentimental and comic, and also the grim tragedies of the Boer war."

Great applause from the audience.

During the performance; the eloquent Theodore made five other speeches, pointing out how interrupters would be dealt with in Ginnett's and Sanger's circus.

"Not only would the hinterrupter be ejected from the theatyer, but the 'ole performance would be abandoned. I, 'owever, am not going to allow the audience who have paid for an entertainment to suffer from the conduct of any hindividual or hindividuals, and, therefore, the programme shall be given in full."

More applause, and then the wonderful magicograph.

"Now ladies and gentlemen," said the irrepressible Theodore, "I am about to show you something that has never yet been exhibited by a travelling company. In one of the pictures you will catch a glimpse of the Boers on the brow of a hill firing on the British in the plains below. This, ladies and gentlemen, is the honly photograph which has ever been taken of the Boers in action."

"Begob, but I believe that's thrue for him,' said Jerry to the sapper. "There's a captain home, invaleded from South Afrikey, staying back on a visit at Master George's at present. Murra, but he has wondherful tales o' the front. I heerd him tell how wan day himself an' the docther an' a gineral was ridin' out from the camp, ridin' along the themselves, it appears, on a tower of pleasure. Well, they was ridin' along when they hears two shots; the reports was so far away that they took no notice, but rode

on continuing their tower o'pleasure, in the direction they was going. They was hardly gone a hundred yards when shlap goes another shot, an' down falls the gineral from between the two o' thim. Murra, the docthor jumped off his horse, an' there he was dead, with a bullet in his heart. The captain wheeled round an' galloped back as hard as he could to the camp, an', hanom-an-deoul, but he was three weeks in bed with the fright av it. After that he got up and did some manoeuvres agin, but he caught that faver an' aguy, an' shure I suppose he let on to be worse than he was, too, for they sint him home on sick lave, and the divil a wan o' him, he says, 'll ever go out agin."

Now, during all this recital the sapper was becoming more and more uneasy and indignant. To add to his ill-humour, something kept pushing itself under the

tent between his feet. Taking it to be a dog, he pushed it away time after time, and finally gave it a very smart kick back wards. There was a savage growl and some whispering outside, and just as Flanagan's story was finished a sod of turf hopped off the tail of the sapper's coat, setting alight a box of matches he carried therein.

The sapper gave a bound in the air; of course there was nobody to be seen.

"Jest loike yer bloomin' Boers," he said to Jerry; "they foires an' they runs away."

"An' be the same token," said Jerry, "I see that ye have yer wounds in the rere."

"What do ye mean?"

"Och, ne'er a ha' porth but jest what I say."

"Now, gentlemen," said the showman, "this can't be allowed; if ye want to fight, why go outside."

After a preliminary tussle and terrible threats on both sides, they went out. Awaiting them was the local sergeant, who ordered them home from the village. As they were rather disinclined to follow his directions, he helped them with a stout blackthorn stick, with such good effect that the argument has never since been resumed.

Joseph K. O'Connor ('Heblon') *Studies in Blue* (Dublin, 1905)

JOSEPH O'CONNOR was a barrister in Dublin whose literary fancy it was to contribute humorous essays to the Dublin Evening Mail. Born in Ashford, Co. Limerick in 1878 most of his essays are about the City.

Military Barracks, Clonmel, Co. Tipperary (Lawrence Collection, National Library)

Killarney Pipe Band, 1912 (MacMonagle Collection Killarney)

TIMOTHY DANIEL SULLIVAN was born in Bantry, Co. Cork in 1827. He had the same kind of journalistic and political career as his brother A. M, representing Westmeath, Donegal and Dublin at Westminster. He was the editor of that nineteeth-century staple of Irish bookshelves, *Speeches from the Dock* and his name will be forever famous as the author, in response to the treatment of the Manchester Martyrs, of 'God Save Ireland', a rather ironical twist this when one considers his conservative-nationalist career. He died in Dublin in 1914.

THOMAS ASHE was the outstanding guerrilla leader who gave the Volunteers their only victory outside Dublin in 1916. He captured four RIC barracks in the Ashbourne district of Co. Dublin and held out until Pearse ordered the general surrender. He died in Mountjoy Jail during forcible-feeding on 15 September 1917. At his funeral three volleys were fired over his grave and Michael Collins uttered just two sentences: 'Nothing additional remains to be said. The volley which we have just heard is the only speech which it is proper to make above the grave of a dead Fenian.'

GOD SAVE IRELAND

High upon the gallows tree
Swung the noble-hearted Three,
By the vengeful tyrant stricken in their bloom;
But they met him face to face,
With the courage of their race,
And they went with souls undaunted to their doom.
"God save Ireland!" said the heroes;
"God save Ireland!" said they all:
"Whether on the scaffold high
"Or the battle-field we die,
"Oh, what matter, when for Erin dear we fall!"

Climbed they up the rugged stair,
Rang their voices out in prayer,
Then with England's fatal cord around them cast,
Close beneath the gallows tree,
Kissed like brothers lovingly,
True to home and faith and freedom to the last.
"God save Ireland!" said they all:
"Whether on the scaffold high
"Or the battle-field we die,
"Oh, what matter, when for Erin dear we fall!"

Never till the latest day
Shall the memory pass away
Of the gallant lives thus given for our land;
But on the cause must go,
Admidst joy, or weal, or woe,
Till we've made our isle a nation free and grand.
"God save Ireland!" say we proudly;
"God save Ireland!" say we all:
"Whether on the scaffold high
"Or the battle-field we die,
"Oh, what matter, when for Erin dear we fall!"

T. D. Sullivan, 'God Save Ireland' from *Songs and Poems*
(Dublin, 1899)

Thomas Ashe (Keogh Collection, National Library)

TOMÁS MacCURTAIN was Lord
Mayor of Cork in 1920 when the
centre of the city was burned and
looted by British troops. He had
been O/C of the Cork Brigade of the
Irish Volunteers in 1916 and was
known to be the head of disaffection
in Munster. On the early morning
of March 20, 1920, plain-clothes men
and uniformed police and military
isolated the area around his house and
at 1.30 am a group of men with
blackened faces burst in and shot him
at the door of his bedroom. The
coroner's verdict was one of wilful
murder against Lloyd George, Lord
French, Chief Secretary MacPherson
and certain officers in the RIC. The
body lay in state at the City Hall,
Cork from Saturday 21 to Sunday 22,
March.

Lying-in-state of Tomás MacCurtain,
Lord Mayor of Cork, March 21, 1920
70 *(Cork Examiner Collection.)*

'I envied him because the society—the Young Italy—that I belong to——'

'Yes?'

'Intrusted him with a work that I had hoped—would be given to me, that I had thought myself—specially adapted for'.

'What work?'

'The taking in of books—political books—from the steamers that bring them—and finding a hiding place for them—in the town——'

'And this work was given by the party to your rival?'

'To Bolla—and I envied him.'

'And he gave you no cause for this feeling? You do not accuse him of having neglected the mission intrusted to him?'

'No, father; he has worked bravely and devotedly; he is a true patriot and has deserved nothing but love and respect from me.'

Father Cardi pondered.

'My son, if there is within you a new light, a dream of some great work to be accomplished for your fellow-men, a hope that shall lighten the burdens of the weary and oppressed, take heed how you deal with the most precious blessing of God. All good things are of His giving; and of His giving is the new birth. If you have found the way of sacrifice, the way that leads to peace; if you have joined with loving comrades to bring deliverance to them that weep and mourn in secret; then see to it that your soul be free from envy and passion and your heart as an altar where the sacred fire burns eternally. Remember that this a high and holy thing, and that the heart which would receive it must be purified from every selfish thought. This vocation is as the vocation of a priest; it is not for the love of a woman, nor for the moment of a fleeting passion; it is *for God and the people; it is now and for ever.'*

'Ah!' Arthur started and clasped his hands; he had almost burst out sobbing at the motto. 'Father, you give us the sanction of the Church! Christ is on our side——'

'My son,' the priest answered solemnly, 'Christ drove the money-changers out of the Temple, for His House shall be called a House of Prayer, and they had made it a den of thieves.'

After a long silence, Arthur whispered tremulously:

'And Italy shall be His Temple when they are driven out——'

He stopped; and the soft answer came back:

' "The earth and the fulness thereof are mine, saith the Lord." '

E. L. Voynich, *The Gadfly* (New York, 1897)

ETHEL LILIAN VOYNICH was born in 1864 in Cork, the daughter of Prof. George Boole whose work in Mathematical Logic led to the development of Set Theory and the Mathematics of Circuity. She married Count Voynich, a Polish emigre, in 1890 and through him was introduced to the Italy about which she had had so many romantic dreams. Mazzini had been the great hero of her girlhood and *The Gadfly* (1897) her greatest novel was set in the time of the *risorgimento*. She died in 1960 at the age of 96 having spent the last forty years of her life in New York.

TERENCE MacSWINEY was born in Cork in 1879. He trained as an accountant and afterwards took a degree in philosophy from the Royal University. He was an enthusiastic supporter of the Gaelic League but was deflected from linguistic concerns when the League went political in 1913. Interned at Frongoch in 1916 he returned to full-time Volunteer activity in 1917. He became Lord Mayor of Cork on the death of Tomas MacCurtain in 1920 but was arrested in the August of that year. His death after seventy days of hunger strike aroused a great deal of emotion. The remains lay in state for a day in Southwark Cathedral. The intention to bring them to Dublin was foiled by the authorities who commandeered them at Holyhead and had them brought to Cork. He was buried in the Republican Plot, Cork after an immense funeral on Sunday, 1 November, 1920.

The Revolutionist was written in 1909 but was not produced until after his death (at the Abbey in 1921). The play in its political philosophy and in its sense of the need for personal, supreme sacrifice is clearly autobiographical.

FOLEY. Yes. Dead.

CON. This hand is warm.

FOLEY. The breath has only just left him.

CON. But there's colour in his face.

FOLEY. It sometimes happens—he died in great pain.

CON. And no one near him.

FATHER O'CONNOR. God never left him.

CON. I can't realize 'tis death. Look at his face.

FOLEY. He's composed now.

FATHER O'CONNOR' He's very beautiful.

> *(Hugh's look is strangely beautiful. The last struggle forced the blood to his face; it has not entirely receded and leaves a colour behind with an effect strangely natural. The lines of pain are smoothed out; his expression is quiet and happy with the trace of a smile. The others stand looking at him in silence. His look acts on them for a moment like a spell. Foley's reference to Nora breaks the spell.)*

FOLEY. She will be coming.

CON. My God, what shall we do?

FOLEY. There may be a delay. She missed me and ran for others.

CON *(to Father O'Connor).* Could you keep her out?

FATHER O'CONNOR. I'll try

FOLEY. There's some one coming.

CON. Quick.

FATHER O'CONNOR. She has courage, thank God. *(Going.)*

CON *(looking on Hugh).* Thank God, he's so beautiful. *(Father O'Connor goes out quickly. Immediately an altercation is heard outside.)*

Terence MacSwiney, *The Revolutionist* (Dublin, 1914)

Funeral of Terence MacSwiney (MacMonagle Collection, Killarney)

'Eighteen Pounder' pictured in the old barrack yard, New Street, Carrick-on-Suir. The officers are Colonel Heslip and Joyce (rank unknown) of the National Army. (Mrs Pike, Carrick Society).

Shaun Foddha was posted, with half-a-dozen others, behind the pile of rocks near Elsie Dhuv's cabin, to at least delay the artillery, in case they should come that way, by rolling large stones down to the narrow roads, and discharging their firearms, such as they were. Of course the tall blacksmith had his blunderbuss—in the efficacy of which he had such perfect faith, that the fully expected to see the King's troops—not to mention the hated but despised yeomanry—recoil in terror and consternation before the first discharge. He contemptuously rejected Chris Carmody's advice to take an old musket, which though rust-eaten outside, and a very shaky weapon, either to handle or to look at, Chris assured him was sound at the breech, and but slightly honeycombed on the inside of the barrel. But Shaun Foddha would not have exchanged his stumpy blunderbuss for the best and newest musket in Europe, or the surest and deadliest rifle that every rang in an American forest. One 'bellus' at the enemy was all Shaun wanted with the blunderbuss, loaded as it was for a week with slugs to the very muzzle.

The chances, however, were but slight that the military would come by the narrow road that crossed Glounsoggarth. Hubert Butler saw this, and collected as many men as he could, and posted them in a grove a mile or two from the bridge in the glen which commanded the wider and more level road at a point where he thought an attack could be successfully made upon the guns, and the carriages broken, so as to enable him to raise the siege of O'Carroll's house by an attack upon the yeomen before they could be reinforced by the regulars, who would require some time to recover from the shock of an unexpected sortie from the grove.

Both Fergus O'Carroll and Captain Branton saw a horseman ride to the crest of the hill opposite the house two or three times, within a couple of hours, and after apparently surveying the ground below, wheel round and disappear down the other side of the hill, but neither the captain nor the rebel chief whom he had entrapped, as he believed, beyond all hope of escape, could form the remotest guess who the inquisitive horseman might be, or whether he was friend or foe, or merely an indifferent looker-on.

That he was not an idle spectator, at all events, was soon apparent, both to the besieged and besieger. The report of an irregular discharge of musketry was borne over the hill, and almost immediately after the horseman appeared again. But instead of retiring, as he had so often done before, on he came, followed by a small but compact body of men who, to his infinite delight, Fergus O'Carroll, looking from the small window in the gable of his barricaded house, saw plainly enough were not regular soldiers. And, seeing that nearly the whole of the Garryroe Corps were posted round the house, he concluded neither could they be yeomanry. The only other possible conclusion was that they were friends. His heart beat quick; for he had really made up his mind to die. In the hurry of the moment he had let Dick Maher down from the window, desiring him to collect as many of the boys as he could, and make some demonstration that might give him a chance of making a rush through the yeomen, who surrounded the house on every side. But when he had time for reflection, he saw the hopelessness of this project.

Charles Kickham *Elsie Dhuv* (Dublin, 1886)

This was the gun used by General Prout of the Free State forces to soften Republican resistance in Waterford from Ferrybank on 19 July 1922. A similar gun had been used to take Limerick earlier in July. Even before Limerick had fallen the Republican general Liam Lynch had drawn back to the mountainous region of South Tipperary around Clonmel and Carrick. Carrick became a Republican headquarters and at one stage De Valera, Childers and Markiewicz operated the government of the Provisional Republic from there. Dinny Lacy and Dan Breen established HQ at the Workhouse with around 500 men. McCarthy, Ryan and Byrne (under Gen. Prout) took Carrick with the 18-pounder on 2 August 1922. As the Republicans withdrew they burnt the local RIC barracks and the courthouse. In the movement up the Suir valley by Prout the gun was used continually to push the Republicans back to Clonmel and thence to the mountains of North Cork.

CHARLES JOSEPH KICKHAM was born in Mullinahone, Co. Tipperary, in 1828. Nationalist journalism which was carried on in spite of congenitally poor hearing and eyesight damaged in a youthful accident led to involvement in Young Ireland and Fenianism. He was on the staff of *The Irish People* when he and John O'Leary were arrested and sentenced to fourteen years imprisonment for involvement in the Fenian Conspiracy. He received the harsh treatment that prison staffs reserved for Fenians but he was less able to withstand it than O'Donovan Rossa and the others. After four years he was released, broken in health and almost totally blind. He died in Blackrock in 1882, three years after the publication of his book, *Knocknagow*, surely the most famous of all 19th-century Irish books.

TO GOD AND IRELAND TRUE.

I sit beside my darling's grave,
    Who in the prison died,
And tho' my tears fall thick and fast,
    I think of him with pride:
Ay, softly fall my tears like dew,
For one to God and Ireland true.

"I love my God o'er all," he said,
    "And then I love my land,
And next I love my Lily sweet,
    Who pledged me her white hand:
To each—to all—I'm ever true;
To God—to Ireland—and to you."

No tender nurse his hard bed smoothed
    Or softly raised his head;
He fell asleep and woke in heaven
    Ere I knew he was dead;
Yet why should I my darling rue?
He was to God and Ireland true.

Oh! 't is a glorious memory;
    I'm prouder than a queen
To sit beside my hero's grave,
    And think on what has been:
And, oh, my darling, I am true
To God—to Ireland—and to you.

Ellen O'Leary, 'To God and Ireland
True' in *Lays of Country, Home and
Friends* (Dublin 1891)

ELLEN O'LEARY was born in Tipperary in 1831. She was an ardent Fenian as befitted the sister of John O'Leary the great philosopher-king of Yeats's 'Romantic Ireland'. She had helped Stephens escape in 1866 but for the fifteen years of her brother's imprisonment and exile she lived quietly at home in Tipperary writing occasional poems for periodicals. in 1887 she moved to Dublin to keep house for her repatriated brother and it was here that she met Yeats, T W Rolleston, 'Eva of the Nation', and the other members of the nationalist-literary salon who gathered round the old patriot. After her death in Cork in 1889 (sixteen years before her brother) her verse was published as *Lays of Country, Home and Friends*— a just description.

Dinny Sadlier, 1920 (Mrs Pike/Carrick Society)

DINNY SADLIER was commandant of 7th Battalion, 3rd Tipperary Brigade, IRA, during the War of Independence. He was accidentally shot dead while on active service in 1921. He was buried secretly in Grangemockler but during the truce he was re-interred in his native place, Drangan. His brother, Michael, was killed in the Civil War.

All Ireland south of the Boyne seemed to be suddenly converted into the training-ground of a rebellious organisation. The young men of the towns and of the more populous country places were openly drilled of nights for armed insurrection. Funds were raised everywhere for the purchase of rifles from Birmingham factories; and the weapons were imported at first without let or hindrance on the part of the constituted authorities, who were too much puzzled and bewildered to take any serious purpose in it. Clubs and associations were formed everywhere for the open teaching and propagation of armed rebellion. Then, when the constituted authorities had time to breathe and to recognise the fact that rebellion was in the air, there set in a season of hurried repressive legislation; and arrests and imprisonments became the common events of every day. As might well be expected in such a season of alarm and of panic, the action of the constituted authorities was often widely indiscriminate; and some of the men, elder and younger, who could best have been relied upon to keep the national movement within reasonable bounds, were among the first to be arrested and put on trial, or sent to prison without any form of serious judicial investigation.

All this was to be expected at such a time of commotion and is common enough in the history of very passionate popular agitation, or at least was common in the history of such agitations during those somewhat distant days; but the immediate result of the course taken by the constituted authorities was to convert from ardent nationalists into avowed rebels many of those who had up to the latest moment, still believed that the misgovernment of Ireland could be remedied by argument and appeal addressed to the intelligence of the ruling classes and to the Imperial Parliament.

Justin McCarthy, *Mononia,* (London, 1901)

Michael Collins, C-in-C National Army, inspecting troops at the Square Newcastle West, Co Limerick, on 11 August 1922. (Photo: W F Knight, Newcastle)

JUSTIN McCARTHY was born in Cork in 1830 but spent the last fifty years of his life in London. His career had the recurring nineteenth-century pattern of journalism, editorship and politics. He led the Nationalist Party after the fall of Parnell until 1896, when he retired from active participation in politics. After his resignation he continued an awesome output of writing, including biography and history. He was editor-in-chief of a ten-volume anthology of Irish Literature produced in Philadelphia in 1904. *Mononia* (1901) is set in Munster during the Smith O'Brien rising of 1848. He died in 1912.

The fall of Newcastle West to the National Army under Brig. James Slattery on 5 August 1922 marked the end of Irregular resistance in W Limerick — N Kerry. It was the culmination of General Patrick Daly's clever strategy which involved sea-borne operations at Fenit and Ballylongford, with a third prong of the attack moving westwards from Adare.

On 9 August Collins set out from Dublin to make a tour of the Limerick command. By the 12 August he had reached Tralee where he received word of Arthur Griffith's death and returned to Dublin immediately. On the 22nd he died in an ambush.

IRA officers, Ennistimon, Co Clare, 1919. (Photo: J Arthur)

Incident during a boycott at Kilshanny Church, Co. Clare
(Photo: Joseph Arthur) ·

Journeys

'St. Senanus knew well what he was about, Masther Willie, whin he turned in there to pray an' do pinnance for his sins,' observed the skipper. 'I'll go bail, if he searched all over Ireland ground, he couldn't find a betther place for makin' his sowl than that very sport. He built eleven fine churches there, to the glory of God an' the honour ov the saints; an' why he stopped at the odd number, an' didn't make it the full dozen, I never could rightly make out, but I suppose he did it for good luck. But though the saint build eleven churches, there are only seven, or what's left ov the seven, to the fore to-day. Ov coorse you know that, sir?'

'Of course I do—sure, I often saw them.'

'Well, sir, there they are, sure enough; the ould ancient ruins ov 'em I mane, for it's only the bare walls that' there now, an' more's the pity, for they say that them churches wor great churches entirely wanst upon a time. Sure, 'tis well known that powers ov people used to come from forrin parts in the ould ancient times to get the larnin in Ireland that they hadn't at home in their own country, an' to be taught the light ov the thrue religion. An' that's why Ireland is called the Island ov Saints an' will be called by the same name as long as her fields are green, an' sure that will be to the ind ov the world. But maybe, Masther Willie, you don't b'lieve what I'm tellin' you?'

'Why should not I believe you? It is an historical fact that many holy and learned men lived in Ireland in old times, when the rest of Europe was sunk in the greatest ignorance and barbarism. Of course I believe you.'

'See that now!' exclaimed Lanty, quite delighted to find that his auditor agreed with him. ''Tis a fine thing, sir, to be talking' wid a knowledgable person, like yourself, instead ov the ignorant galloots that's goin' now-a-days.'

KILRUSH on the lower Shannon estuary had an old maritime tradition. There was a regular trade up the estuary from the outport of Cappa to Limerick. The better-off citizens of Limerick travelled on summer holidays to the seaside resort of Kilkee via Cappa. (At first they completed the journey by side-car but after 1892 they used the newly built South Clare Railway.) Cappa also had a coast-guard station, while Scattery Island, a short distance offshore, was the centre from which ships navigating the Shannon took on pilots.

Below: Cappa Pier, Kilrush c.1910 (Lawrence Collection, National Library) The naval gentleman is Michael Pryle the coastguard.

an' if you'll b'lieve me, sir, I'd as lieve be breakin' stones for a pavior as holdin' discourse wid wan ov 'em.'

'But the story, Lanty! you forget that I'm waiting for the story of all this time.'

'Sure enough, sir, but plase the piper you won't have to wait for it long. Did you ever hear ov how St. Senanus or S. Sinan, as we call him for shortness, was converted, an' why it was that he came all the ways to Scatthery Island to do great pinnance for his sins, an' to prove to all the world how greatly he hated women?'

'No, Lanty, I never heard it, but would be very glad to hear it now from you.'

'Arrah, sir! sure a Protestan' like you wouldn't give in at all to such ould shanahus.'

'I don't see what religion has to do with it, one way or other. I hope a Protestant may be allowed to hear a good story, and to enjoy it too, as well as the people who differ from him in creed. So begin at once, Lanty; I am sure you will do the story justice.'

Margaret W Brew, *The Burtons of Dunroe* (London, 1880)

MARGARET BREW lived in Co. Clare, probably near Kilrush and is known mainly as the author of two very popular books, *Chronicles of Castle Cloyne* (1886) and *The Burtons of Dunroe* (1880). Her phonetic rendering of West Clare speech looks odd but her writings have an authenticity which makes them well worth reading even today.

Below: Scattery Island, Kilrush c.1890 (Lawrence Collection, National Library)

The coach of the Cork and Bally-cotton Motor Service Co. Ltd, South Mall, Cork, proprietor J.R. Cross. In inclement weather passengers could keep dry by means of a hood on rails which ran the entire length of the coach. Price of a return trip - four shillings and ninepence.
(*Photo; courtesy J Cluskey*)

A Clare currach is a boat of almost the lightest construction, but it will carry twenty people. In build it is clumsy and shapeless-looking. It has neither keel nor keelson. Like a Dutch galliot, its stem and stern are round; like the craft they call a prong or prom in the south and west of Ireland, its bow and stem rise out of the water, and when under way it skims over the waves rather than cuts through them. On the Shannon and other rivers, the prong is chiefly used for shooting rapids. It has a flat bottom and flat bow, and by this bow being raised out of the water there is less danger of the craft swamping when it rushes headlong into the white foam.

The long heavy swells of the Atlantic on this coast are so many rapids to be climbed and shot, and the light tarred canvas currach, with its round blunt bows and its unresisting keelless bottom, enabling it to be spun swiftly this way or that to meet the eddying sweep, is found to be the safest and most serviceable model. Two men can carry it with ease, but not more than one man in all Killard could by himself lift it and carry it, arms up, and this one man was Edward Martin. All the villagers had seen him do it.

Two years before this morning a bet was made. A number of fishermen subscribed twenty shillings, and laid the money against him. He, the best of fishermen in Killard, put down his pound, raised the currach in his huge arms, and carried it aloft five hundred yards amid the cheers of all, of even those who had lost.

When he lowered the currach, he sat down on it to rest and wipe his flushed, steaming face. Pat Casey, who had arranged the bets and held the money, came to him, and, stretching out his hand, said cordially:

The Harbour, Liscannor, Co. Clare - (Lawrence Collection, National Library)

Flagstones were exported from Liscannor to many British cities where they were used for paving. (The Royal Mint in London was floored with Moher flag.) Nine companies in all worked four quarries, at Doonagore, Caherbarna, Luogh and Moher. The largest was at Doonagore around which a sizable village grew and the stone was taken the four miles from that quarry by good metalled road to Liscannor. The wagons were drawn by the steam engine to the berth of the 'County Clare', the company's ship. The first world war, political change and concrete put an end to the trade.

'Well done, Edward Martin! You won fairly, and deserve the money. Take it, for no other man in this parish, or the next one to it, could do the like of that.'

Martin did not reach out his hand, but continued to wipe his face and neck.

'Take your money, man!' cried Casey, in a tone of expostulation. Casey knew Martin did not like the idea of the bet.

Martin turned to his wife, who stood beside him. She was weeping for joy at the triumph of her husband.

'You would not think,' she was saying to her heart, 'that he had the strength to raise an oar when he takes our little Mary in his arms; and look at what he has done to-day! But strong as his arms are, his love is stronger, and his goodness as strong as ever was goodness in man. My husband!'

At the crowning thought that he was hers, she gave a sob of gratitude, and, sitting down beside him, put her arm on his great shoulder, just as he turned to speak to her.

'Mary,' he said, 'take the money, you. Take the money from Pat Casey, and I'll tell you what to do with it by-and-by.'

Richard Dowling *The Mystery of Killard* (London, 1879)

RICHARD DOWLING was born in Clonmel in 1846. After work as a shipping-clerk in Waterford which gave him an interest in the sea and a taste for nautical yarns that he never lost, he took to journalism. He edited the comic journals *Ireland's Eye* and *Zozimus.* In 1874 he went to London and lived by freelancing for the many magazines which were published in that golden age of popular journalism. He died in 1898. *The Mystery of Killard* is pure Irish Gothic with an anti-hero who is a deaf-mute and who hates his own normally equipped child. The setting is the sea-coast of Clare, near Bishop's Island.

If Jack Creedon did not get to where the road from Carrignadoura crosses the road to Acharas in time to catch up the mail car — well, he would have to walk the whole long ten miles into Raheen, to walk them every step instead of sitting, neighbour-like, on the car chatting to Larry O'the driver. With him Jack Creedon loved to chat — that is when Larry could be got to speak at all. For the most part he spoke only to his horse.

Above an edge of the hill he presently saw the tail-board of Larry's car; the car was not moving, a thing that made him wonder. And soon he saw Larry himself, a little away from his horse, stamping about on the watery road. His hands were deep in his pockets, his whip was gripped under his elbow, and his face was looking more crusty than ever. There he was stamping about on the mountain-top, impatience itself. A twikle came into Jack Creedon's eye. He could make no guess at what was causing Larry to delay in so windy a spot after driving through miles of rain; he did not try to guess; the vision before him was sufficient, he enjoyed it, and he knew he would treasure it up in his memory. He raised his voice:

"Eh." he cried, "is it taking the air ye are?"

Old Larry turned.

"The air!" he snarled.

"Ye might be civil — Is it anyone ye're waiting for?"

"Him!" Without taking his hands from his pockets Larry twisted himself until his whip pointed towards a series of striplike rocks that rose to a fine view-point. There Jack Creedon saw a well-dressed stranger staring intently over the streaming valley into the sunset. Its glare had caused him to put his hand above his eyes.

"Who is he?" whispered Jack.

"One of them tourists — leave me alone!"

Then Jack made a motion towards the car; would he mount? Larry surlily nodded; and without causing the crazy old thing to creak in a joint or spring, Jack Creedon got up on it and bided his time. Meanwhile old Larry stamped on the wet rocks.

The sunset soon parted with its glory; the sky grew cold and livid, the clouds became the colour and shape of dusky wings. Turning from it, the American silently made for his seat in the car. He took in the new passenger with a soft glance amd slow nod.

Dusk thickened; night fell as they swung along the slopes of the interminable hills. They would climb slowly up a long rise, the stroke of every hoof echoing from the rocks above their heads. Then, a quick change, they swung down the descent at a reckless pace, the car swaying from side to side.

Daniel Corkery, *A Munster Twilight* (Dublin, 1916) Library)

Long car outside Lake Hotel, Inchigeela, Co. Cork
(Lawrence Collection, National Library)

DANIEL CORKERY was born in Cork in 1878 and as teacher, critic and author helped to confirm the respectable existence of an Anglo-Irish literature which he professionally decried. His novels and stories are provincial in the deepest and best sense of that word. An able pamphleteer for the Gaelic League, his general criticism suffered from an understandable but debilitating anti-Englishness. He died in 1964.

'In the twenty-one miles between Glengarriff and Kenmare one does not see a score of dwellings. How do the inhabitants of these wretched huts make a living? During the season they live on the mendicity of their children. You cannot go half a mile without an escort of both sexes and all ages, indescribably ragged, trotting barefoot in the wind around the vehicle, and offering you bouquets of heather, bunches of moss and sprays of bog-myrtle. This goes on the whole way. For a quarter of an hour there may be a respite, then a new band emerges from some ditch, and you are thus handed over from brigade to brigade until you reach your destination.'
Madame de Bovet, *Three months in Ireland* (London, 1891)

Gap Cottage, Killarney
(Lawrence Collection, National Library)

89

"Talkin' about railways," said my friend Pat Hurley to me one July evening, as he sat in the little garden in front of his cottage, "I could tell you a quare wan." Now we were not talking about railways, though we could have found plenty to say about this particular line, which runs from Cork "to the back of God-speed"; we were watching the train go out from a little country station in the South of Ireland. My friend was a porter on the same line, but just at present was on sick-leave for a few days. His tongue was as the pen of a ready writer; and, conscious of his powers as a story-teller, he kept his eyes and ears open for everything which added to his fund of entertainment.

"If ye'll give me lave to light me pipe, sir, I can tell ye something that'll divart ye."

I graciously granted his request, and as he filled a very decent-looking briar he began:

"Och, if Jim Walsh only heard what I'm talkin' about he'd murther me, for the same matther made a hullabaloo in the town, and the laugh that was riz agin the two of us ye never heard the like; not but many of thim that was laughing didn't know betther theirselves. Wan evenin' when we was clanin' out the carriages afther the thrain was in, we come on the quarest-lookin' tin box; the like of it we never sot an eye on before. There was nathar mark nor token on it to tell a body who owned it.

" 'Bedad, that's the onhandiest-lookin' luggage I iver see,' sez Jim.

" ' 'Tis so,' says I, 'an' powerful heavy,' takin' a grip of it an' haulin' it out on the platform.

"There was only three ladies in that carriage, an' in coorse it had to belong to wan o' thim. We argued it somethin' mighty particular from the quare shape of it, let alone belongin' to wan o' the quality, so I conthrived to persuade Jim that 'twas the dacint thing to take it home to the craythur, an' lave it wid her that night before she'd be feelin' the want of it. Poor Jim is a very soft-hearted kind of bhoy, an' being younger and smarter than me, he shouldhered the conthrapshin and sthreeled off. Troth, he was back in an hour's time, an' the box wid him.

" 'Be jabers,' sez he, 'me back's bruk; ye might as well offer to carry the pyramids of Agypt.' He sot down wake like and wiped the seat off his face an' round his

neck wid his cap.

" 'Why didn't ye get shut of it?' sez I.

" 'Sure,' sez he, 'ye must be thinkin' it's for an ornament I'm wearing it; divil a wan o' thim would own up to it at all. I took it first to Miss Mary Murphy, an' she was at her tay, but she sent me out word that she had all her thraps right. I wint on thin to Mrs. Barry, an' afther her Mrs. Kelly. I was mistook wid thim too, bedad, for they was only in Cork for the day, an' they had no luggage that you might call luggage. I was bate entirely carryin' what might be a quarry o' stones for the weight, an' leppin' wid rage for havin' to do it. I thraced my steps back to Miss Mary Murphy, she being' the likeliest of the three faymales, an' toult the girl for God's sake to ax her misthress to have a look at the box, if it wouldn't be throublin' her honor, for I was heart-scalded wid dhraggin' it over land an' say. Miss Mary couldn't talk to me at wanst, be rayson o' company in the parlor, but she sint ordhers that I was to

come in an' rest meself, the Lord bless her kind heart. She's a raal lady, is Miss Mary Murphy; there's not her aqual in the town. She sint me out a dhrink o' porter; bedad I was glad to get a hoult of it, an' whin I had me fingers on the glass I was ready to face the ould bhoy. After a bit Miss Mary come out, an' took wan look at me weight o' calamity, an' thin she laughed fit to shplit her stays.

" 'Och, Jim,' sez she, 'but ye're the omadhaun.'

" 'For the love o' the Blessed Vargin, Miss,' sez I, 'say ye own this misfortunit thrunk.'

" 'I don't,' sez she, 'but I know who does.'

" 'Thin tell me,' sez i, very polite, 'where the blazes am I to take it to?'

" 'I'd advise ye,' sez she, 'to take it to the Lost Property Office in Cork,' an' wid that she roared out laughin' agin an' ran away. I could hear 'em all inside screechin' at the fun, whatever it was. So I shouldhered the moniment wanst more, an' here I am.

Sophie MacIntosh, 'Jim Walsh's Tin Box' in *Irish Literature* VI (Philadelphia, 1904)

SOPHIE MacINTOSH was born in Kinsale as Sophie Donaclift. She married H F MacIntosh who became headmaster of Methodist College, Belfast. Her school stories were published in 1902 as *The Last Forward*. *Jim Walsh's Tin Box* is typical of her uncomplicated approach to her fellow Cork people.

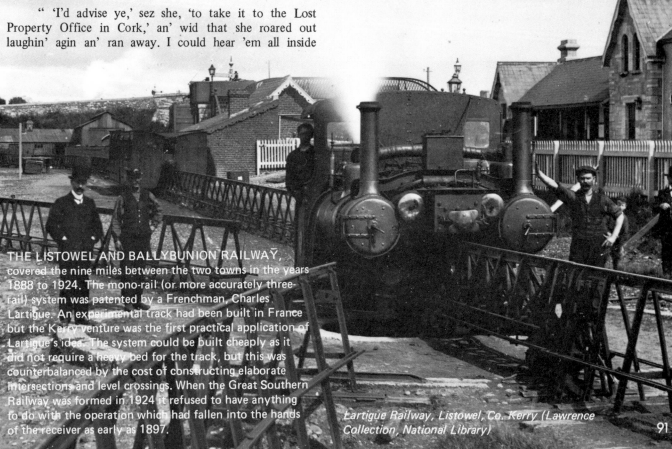

THE LISTOWEL AND BALLYBUNION RAILWAY, covered the nine miles between the two towns in the years 1888 to 1924. The mono-rail (or more accurately three-rail) system was patented by a Frenchman, Charles Lartigue. An experimental track had been built in France but the Kerry venture was the first practical application of Lartigue's idea. The system could be built cheaply as it did not require a heavy bed for the track, but this was counterbalanced by the cost of constructing elaborate intersections and level crossings. When the Great Southern Railway was formed in 1924 it refused to have anything to do with the operation which had fallen into the hands of the receiver as early as 1897.

Lartigue Railway, Listowel, Co. Kerry (Lawrence Collection, National Library)

FAREWELL

Sail bravely on, thou gallant bark,
   Across the Western sea;
And safely guard the precious freight
   Thou bear'st away from me.
Sail on, nor heed the frowning skies,
   Nor angry wave nor wind;
Nor reck the grief of aching hearts
   Thou leavest here behind.

Great God! Protector of the world,
   Guard Thou both wife and child.

Like miser watching from the shore
   The argosy that bears
O'er ocean paths to distant lands
   The treasures prized of years,
I sit and graze, through streaming eyes,
   Across the darkening main,
And fain would have the good ship turn
   And bring back again.

Sail on, brave ship; a priceless stake
   Is on thy fate for me!
May angels waft thee on thy course,
   And calm each threatening sea!
Sancta Maria! to thy care
   Are child and mother given,
Whether we meet again on earth,
   Or meet our next in heavn!

A. M. Sullivan 'Farewell' in *Irish Literature* (Philadelphia, 1904)

ALEXANDER MARTIN SULLIVAN was born in Castletownberehaven, Co. Cork in 1830 and broke into literature, so to speak, when he bought *The Nation* from the severely disenchanted Charles Gavan Duffy in 1858. Mingled careers of politics and journalism made his name and that of his brother TD well-known throughout England and Ireland. His *Story of Ireland*, a colourful, romantic history written in 1870 became very popular and was admired, among others, by Winston Churchill. His poems and songs were published mainly in *The Nation*. He died in Dublin in 1884.

Lusitania (Cork Examiner)

COBH, one of the great victims of the Gaelic Revival, was known decently enough as the Cove of Cork until 2 August 1849 when the visit of Victoria, Albert and their four young children caused the city fathers to change the name to Queenstown. Complaints about facilities encouraged by the royal visit led to the building of the Victoria Quay. It remained unsalubrious as at least one sensitive traveller noted:

'Should it ever be my happy lot to revisit the city and haven of Cork, I shall most certainly decline to land at Queenstown. The gentleman who took a census of the smells of Cologne might perhaps be interested in this locality and would find an ample field for his nasal arithmetic. The heat was intense, the tide low; and though I have no doubt that, farther from the sea, the place is sweet and healthy enough, I never remember to have inhaled so offensive an atmosphere as that which prevailed . . . in the front street of Queenstown.' S Reynolds Hole, *A Little Tour of Ireland* (London, 1896)

INDEX OF AUTHORS

Brew M 83
Buckley W 8
Conyers D 13
Corkery D 88, 89
Cronin W ('Liam') 57
Crottie J 18
Cummins G & Day S 26
De Vere A 59
Dowling R 87
Fitzmaurice G 8, 30
Hogan M 8, 62
Joyce R D 40, 41
Kelleher D L 54
Kickham C 8, 75
Laffan M 10
Lane D 53
Langbridge R 51
MacIntosh S 91
MacNamara M A 16
MacSwiney T 72
McAuliffe E F 24
McCarthy J 78, 79
McCarthy M J F 23
Murray T C 8, 14
O'Brien W 8, 37
O'Connor J K ('Heblon') 67
Ó Criomhthain T 60, 61
O'Donovan J 44
Ó Dúbhghaill S
   (Beirt Fhear) 47
Ó hAodha T 11
O'Leary E 76
Robinson L 8, 34
Sheehan P A 8, 64
Somerville E & Ross M 8
Sullivan A M 8, 92
Sullivan T D 8, 68, 69
Synge J M 20
Thurston K C 8, 38
Voynich E L 71

Acknowledgements

For kind permission to reprint copyright material the following acknowledgements are made: to the Dolmen Press for George Fitzmaurice; William Heinemann for E L Voynich; John Farquharson Ltd for Somerville and Ross; and Gill and Macmillan Ltd for William Cronin.

For kind permission to use photographs acknowledgements are made: to the National Library of Ireland; the Cork Examiner; the Crawford Municipal School of Art, Cork; Harry McKnight; the Carrick Society; Edmond Flaherty; Sean MacGinnea; Don MacMonagle; M J Glynn.

Select Bibliography
S J Brown. *Ireland in Fiction*. Dublin, 1919.
D J O'Donoghue. *The Poets of Ireland*. Dublin, 1912.
B T Cleeve. *Dictionary of Irish Writers*. Cork 1967-1971.
M Brown. *The Politics of Irish Literature*. London, 1971.
M Gorham. *Ireland From Old Photographs*. London, 1971.
K Hickey. *The Light of Other Days*. London, 1973.
P Flanagan. *Transport in Ireland 1880-1910*. Dublin, 1969
F S L Lyons. *Ireland since the Famine*. London, 1973.

Golf Hotel, Harbour View, Bandon (Lawrence Collection, National Library)